MARK CROW

MASTERING YOUR STORMS

Navigating the Trials of Life Effectively

HONOR✦NET
THE HONOR NETWORK

Mark Crow writes with refreshing candor about the inevitable storms of life, yet his focus is never on the storm but on the Savior who comes to see us safely through. Written out of his own experiences with life's storms and God's faithfulness, Mastering Your Storms *is honest, practical, and faith filled.*

—Richard Exley, author of *The Alabaster Cross, Encounters with Christ, Man of Valor,* and *Witness the Passion*

All of us go through tough times in our lives, but it is comforting to know that we don't have to face them alone. These words of my friend, Mark Crow, will masterfully help you understand that God is with you in the storms, even when the dark clouds make it difficult to see Him. As you learn to trust God, you will discover that you can master the storms in your life when you are firmly anchored to the One who is the bedrock of your faith. This powerful book will bless and encourage you—and all of God's people— helping you to experience His peace...even in the midst of the storm.

—Dr. Doug Carter, Senior Vice President, EQUIP, John C. Maxwell, Founder

Mark Crow illustrates in his new book, Mastering Your Storms, *that all will experience life's trials and tribulations. But our response to these storms can define our true character and show the loving, faithful heart of God in any circumstance. Pastor Crow has a true gift of speaking to people about God's plan for their lives and God's healing touch.*

> —Mary Fallin, Lieutenant Governor,
> Oklahoma

Refreshing and real! Mark Crow's transparency and practicality offer the reader the opportunity to experience true healing and growth. This anointed teaching is life-giving to everyone who is in the midst of a storm.

> —Mark Lewandowski, Ph.D.
> Dean of School of Business,
> Oral Roberts University

Special Thanks

Thanks to my wife, Jennifer, for twenty-five years of faithfully going through the great times as well as the storms of life with me. You have helped me to stay on course.

Thanks to my five wonderful children—Chris, Evangeline, Andrew, Joseph, and Victoria—for being so flexible on life's journey. I know that it hasn't always been easy, but it has been fun. Life would not be the same without each and every one of you. You are the greatest gift, next to salvation, that God has given to your mother and me. You are the best. I love you more than you will ever be able to comprehend.

Thanks to my staff for riding out many storms with me; you trusted me to lead even during the times when I wasn't sure what was ahead. It is a privilege to be your pastor and your friend.

Thanks to my church family at Victory Church, Oklahoma City, Norman, Corpus Christi, and Victory Iglesia. Your prayers and confidence have made it possible for me to put this message into print. You are the greatest. I love you.

Fourth printing, February 2009
Copyright © 2006—Mark Crow
Mastering Your Storms—Navigating the Trials of Life Effectively

ISBN 0-9753036-5-1
ISBN 978-0-9753036-5-8
Printed in the United States of America.

Published by HonorNet
P.O. Box 910
Sapulpa, OK 74067
Web site: honornet.net

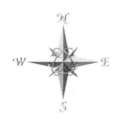

CONTENTS

FOREWORD

I'm honored to write a foreword for *Mastering Your Storms*. Each time I visit Pastor Mark Crow and his wonderful church, I leave refreshed. Pastor Mark is an amazing leader, communicator, husband, father, and friend, but most importantly, he lives with enthusiasm and joy in serving God.

> *For though a righteous man falls seven times, he rises again.*
>
> —Proverbs 24:16, NIV

This message you hold was not birthed in a laboratory devoid of personal experience; it was birthed through storms and trials. Each of us goes through

storms. Each of us has made mistakes. It is our response
to these challenges that positions us. I encourage you
to open your heart as you read and look not only at the
message but beyond to God Himself. There you will
find strength and wisdom to navigate even the fiercest
storms of life. Mark Crow has a word for our generation and a heart to see others succeed in this life and
throughout eternity.

—John Bevere, Author/Speaker
Co-founder of Messenger International
Colorado Springs, Australia,
United Kingdom

Dear friends, do not be surprised at the painful trial you are suffering, as though something strange were happening to you.

—1 Peter 4:12

"In this world you will have trouble. But take heart! I have overcome the world."

—John 16:33

INTRODUCTION

STORMS ARE INEVITABLE IN OUR NATURAL WORLD. Some blow through relatively quickly, bringing down a few branches in the front yard. Other storms, like the ones we're famous for here in Oklahoma, can leave a terrifying path of destruction in their wake.

Storms are inevitable in our personal worlds as well. Jesus promised His followers, "In this world you will have trouble." Why then are we so often surprised when the storms come—especially the ones that tear through our lives, threatening to destroy us?

The Church does a great job telling new believers about all the blessings and victories they will experience now that they are followers of Christ. But maybe we don't do as good a job telling them about the storms they will still have to face—or *how* to face them. Even Christians of many years can be broadsided by an unexpected, furious squall: company downsizing, marital infidelity, illness, death. We live in a fallen world. That means we live in a sinful world where people do not behave as we would like—sometimes even those we most love—and where our bodies are prone to disease and, yes, sometimes death.

As Christians, we know that we also have an enemy, one who comes to rob, kill, and destroy. The Scripture tells us that the enemy will come in like a flood (see Isaiah 59:19). How then can we withstand the flood and not be destroyed?

I pray that as you read this book, you will find the answer to that question—information that will give you the ability to face the storms of your life, no matter what they are, without fear. To come through the storms without being injured. And to arrive on the other side with something to give those who are waiting there who need you.

INTRODUCTION

You see, it isn't enough for those of us who love Jesus to simply survive the storm, to get washed up on the beach, exhausted, beat up, and ready for early retirement. No, there are people waiting on the other side of your storm who need the faith you are bringing.

But Jesus didn't just promise that we would have storms—He also told us He would never leave us or forsake us as we walked through them. To that end, He has left us both a guide, the Holy Spirit, and a guidebook, His Scripture. I want to share with you what I have learned from following His Spirit and His Word in facing my own storms, and in walking alongside many other Christians in the midst of theirs.

Finally, I want you to be able to say not just, "I made it through," but, "I made it through that terrible storm and came out stronger, with the joy of the Lord, more in love with the Lord, and ready for the next step He has planned for my life." So walk with me now as we learn how to face our storms without fear, how to stay on course during those storms, and how to keep the wind of the Spirit in our sails.

"Therefore everyone who hears these words of mine and puts them into practice is like a wise man who built his house on the rock. The rain came down, the streams rose, and the winds blew and beat against that house, yet it did not fall, because it had its foundation on the rock."

—Matthew 7:24-25

CHAPTER ONE

THE STORMS WILL COME

RICK WARREN SAID, "LIFE IS A SERIES OF problems: either you are in one now, you're just coming out of one or you're getting ready to go into another one. The reason for this is that God is more interested in your character than your comfort. God is more interested in making your life holy than He is in making your life happy. We can be reasonably happy here on earth, but that's not the goal of life. The goal is to grow in character, in Christlikeness... I used to think that life was hills and valleys—you go through a dark time, then you go to the mountaintop, back and forth. I don't believe that anymore. Rather than life being hills and valley, I believe that it's kind of like two rails on a railroad track, and at all times you have something good and something bad in your life. No matter how good things are in your life, there is always something bad that needs to be worked on. And no matter how bad things are in your life, there is always something good you can thank God for."[1]

God's Word is always honest. He always tells the truth. He tells us we will *face trials of many kinds* (James 1:2), but He also says, *no one would be unsettled by these trials* for we are *destined* to experience them (1 Thessalonians 3:3). He prepares us by saying, *"In this world you will have trouble"* (John 16:33).

We don't have to live very long to experience the truth of these predictions. Trials come at us in many forms: financial problems, marital problems, kid problems, health problems. Some of these problems hit us

---

[1]This excerpt was taken from *Decision* magazine, November 2004; © 2004 Billy Graham Evangelistic Association; used by permission, all rights reserved.

with the force of an F-5 tornado, scattering the pieces of our lives like so much storm debris. Sometimes it seems like we're going through a season of storms, one right after another, until we are gasping for breath.

God's Word didn't predict just the trials, however. He has given us precious promises of His presence and His help and insight into His purpose in all the storms of our lives. But how do we take hold of these promises? How can we take them into our hearts, so that we can face our storms with confidence in God, and come out on the other side without our lives being twisted or destroyed, but stronger and with something to give to those who need us?

TWO KINDS OF STORMS

There are two kinds of storms. The first kind is what I call the *external storms*. These are storms of circumstances, if you will: from our jobs, our relationships, our finances, and our physical bodies. While we might contribute to these storms by our bad choices, these storms are still largely the result of living in a fallen world.

But there's another kind of storm—what I call *internal storms*. These are caused by wrong thinking about our external storms. Internal storms are created when we respond with anger, bitterness, or resentment to whatever external storm is swirling around us. We begin to develop wrong thinking about ourselves— our past and our future—and about our relationship to God. These internal storms are the most destructive.

So while we can acknowledge the inevitability of the external storms of this life, how do we keep them from getting on the inside of us, where they do the most damage?

EXTERNAL AND INTERNAL STORMS

In Matthew 7, Jesus gives us a picture of two men in the midst of a storm. One of them keeps the storm on the outside, and the other lets it destroy him:

> *"Therefore everyone who hears these words of mine and puts them into practice is like a wise man who built his house on the rock. The rain came down, the streams rose, and the winds blew and beat against that house; yet it did not fall, because it had its foundation on the rock. But everyone who hears these words of mine and does not put them into practice is*

like a foolish man who built his house on sand. The rain came down, the streams rose, and the winds blew and beat against that house, and it fell with a great crash."

—Matthew 7:24-27

Here Jesus gives us some simple but profound counsel: If we will take into our hearts His words, and if we will put them into practice in our lives, we will not be crushed by our trials and tragedies.

I want to give you some storm-tested, scriptural principles that if put into practice as Jesus says, will keep you from falling. *"No weapon formed against you shall prosper"* (Isaiah 54:17 NKJV), and no storm will destroy your faith or your confidence in God.

SIX PRINCIPLES FOR MASTERING YOUR STORMS

Here are six principles you can use to help master your storms. When hard times come, these simple, fundamental truths will see you through.

1. Reach out and in

Why *reach out*? Because the Bible says, *in the multitude of counselors there is safety* (Proverbs 11:14 NKJV). There is safety in knowing and hearing from other believers when you're in the midst of overwhelming difficulties. We usually don't do our best thinking or feel the strongest faith during these times, so don't let pride and embarrassment imprison you. Let someone who has a strong core confidence in God speak into your life and your circumstance.

Paul writes to the Thessalonians after their church had come under terrible persecution: *We sent Timothy, who is our brother and God's fellow worker in spreading the gospel of Christ, **to strengthen and encourage you in your faith,** so that no one would be unsettled by these trials* (1 Thessalonians 3:2-3, emphasis added).

Why is there *safety* in reaching out? We know that [our] *enemy the devil prowls around like a roaring lion looking for someone to devour* (1 Peter 5:8). He wants to isolate you from the flock of God and from the Shepherd. When you are off by yourself, you become an easy target for his attack—his lies, discouragement, and accusations.

Reaching out is not the first action we often take in a storm, however. As I said, our thinking gets confused, and sometimes we begin to believe we created the storm. "If only I hadn't made that decision." "If only I hadn't been so stupid." "If only I had known." "I should be able to handle this."

In my own life as a pastor, I have had to learn to reach out. The years 2002 to 2004 were the most difficult of my life, my marriage, and my twenty-eight years of serving Jesus. Little did my wife, Jennifer, and I know when we began building Victory Church that she would be leveled by a series of major illnesses resulting in chronic fatigue and extended bed rest. And not only were we building a church, we were remodeling our farmhouse as well. And we have five children—the youngest of whom was then four!

Pastors often think they're supposed to be invincible. I used to think that if I could hide my flaws and convince my church that I didn't have any, I might be able to lead them. But coming through that storm taught me that it is not the pastors without flaws who can lead. We must be able to lead in spite of our flaws and during our times of crisis.

I discovered that I had to reach out and seek counsel from Christians I trusted. I sought out those people—and still do today—and said, "I do not know how to handle this. Can you help me?" Their wisdom and their faith encouraged me and built up my own faith.

The external storms become internal ones when we retreat or withdraw into our self-made storm shelters. We mistakenly believe that we will find safety there. But this is not the "safety" we need. We need strength. We need faith. We need confidence in God.

We are already in a place of safety. Psalm 91:2 says that God himself *"is my refuge and my fortress."* And in verse 1, *He who dwells in the shelter of the Most High will rest in the shadow of the Almighty.* We need to get this truth on the inside of us. And sometimes we need to reach out to others who can help us do it.

What about the reaching *in* part?

We must reach deep within our souls to find out what we can do for ourselves to keep from feeling victimized by the storm. It is easy and tempting to fix all our attention on the causes of the storms—which sometimes may be people—but the causes are only part of the problem. Besides, you can only fix yourself. Even if someone has wronged you, or the cause was not of your own making, you must still find the strength inside yourself and in God to deal with the storm. Your ability to reach inside yourself and, hopefully, find faith in the midst of the disaster, is critical.

Sometimes we reach deep within and find something other than faith. Flying home from India in 2000, my jet ran into terrible turbulence. It was a terrifying experience that prompted me to start calling out to God to calm the external storm. After hours of quoting scriptures like *"Peace, be still"* (Mark 4:39 NKJV), with no result, I became convinced that God was up to something. Finally, by looking inside myself, I realized that I was reacting out of fear instead of faith. By reaching inside, I found my answer.

Don't pray that the storm will decrease, but that your faith will increase. Storms, if approached in the right manner, will help you find strength from God.

2. Do routine things

Once you have reached out and reached in, *do the routine things you know to do*. Sleep well. Eat well. Rest. Continue to worship, continue to pray, and continue to read the Word.

When Jesus speaks about *"everyone who hears these words of mine and puts them into practice"* (Matthew 7:24), He is saying that those who continually do what they have heard will see a positive result. Their houses will be built upon the rock and will weather the storm.

The devil wants to get us out of the proper rhythm of living so that we don't eat right or sleep right, and we don't worship, pray, or read our Bibles. The storm cannot move us, however, if we anchor ourselves by practicing these routine things. It can batter us, and even blow some debris into our thinking, but it cannot destroy us.

During that terrible two-year period when Jennifer was so ill, I didn't feel like praying. I didn't feel like building a church—sometimes I didn't even feel like going to church! I often didn't feel like preaching or running a staff. But since when did we start living our lives based solely on our feelings?

Christianity is not based on our emotions. God's Word is still objectively true whether we subjectively feel like it is at any given moment or not. As Christians, we are called to be disciples of Christ. The word *disciple* is related to the word *discipline*. You and I cannot be disciples without having discipline—a continual, obedient response to God's Word.

In her book, *Secure in God's Everlasting Arms*, Elisabeth Elliot gives an illustration from Acts 27, of the benefit of doing the routine things in the midst of a terrifying storm:

When Paul was sailing as a prisoner to Italy and was about to be wrecked in the Adriatic Sea, everyone on board was terror-stricken. Sailors were trying to escape, the soldiers and centurion and captain were all sure they were doomed, and no one paid attention to Paul's assurances of faith in God. But when he suggested that they eat, and actually took bread himself and gave thanks for it, "they were all encouraged and ate some food… and when they had eaten enough, they lightened the ship, throwing the wheat into the sea." [2]

Elisabeth Elliot is probably best known for her book, *Through Gates of Splendor*, the biography of her late husband, Jim Elliot. Jim was one of five missionaries who were killed by the Acua Indians in the jungles of Ecuador. Perhaps you don't know that Elliot was widowed a second time, losing her second husband to cancer. This is what she wrote two months after his death:

> I find that routine is the best support for my soul. I can function with almost my customary efficiency and concentration, so long as I operate by habit—the sameness, ordinariness, and necessity are comforting. It is in the interruption of my routine that I find myself beginning to disintegrate and turn inward. This is hazardous, and I have to take the reins firmly and say "*giddap!*"[3]

In the midst of my own difficulties, I told God that I didn't want to do the routine things of my life, but He just encouraged me to keep on doing the things He had called me to do. In the year following Jennifer's illness, our church grew by a thousand people.

If you keep on doing the things God has called you to do—even in the midst of your storm—what you are communicating to God is faith. Your actions are communicating your trust in His keeping power, even if your feelings are screaming something else. And the storm will stay on the outside.

3. Don't take on the storms of others

Have you noticed that whenever you find yourself in a storm, everyone else who has a storm finds you? You are going through hell, and all of a sudden there's a team that wants to go with you or invites you to go with them! It's almost as though you've become magnetic. Unfortunately, they want to take you through their hells too.

But there are storms that are not yours, so *do not take on the storms of other people*. There is a difference between taking on someone's storm and taking on some-one's need. Someone may have a practical need, and may need your love and your prayers. These are needs you can meet without taking on their storms.

The kind of storm you must avoid—must run for your life from—is someone else's internal storm. Remember, these are the storms that people bring on by wrong thinking about themselves, their circumstance, and about God. These are the storms of bitterness, resentment, and rage. The Word says, *See to it that no...bitter root grows up to cause trouble and defile many* (Hebrews 12:15). In the midst of your external storm, do not let someone else's anger become your anger or someone else's unforgiveness become your unforgiveness. Because then you have let the external storm get on the inside where it will ravage your soul.

As I said in the first principle, reach out to those who will build up your faith. But do not allow the storms of others to get inside your soul.

4. In all things give thanks

The best way to avoid becoming entangled by someone else's bitterness—or your own—is to have a grateful heart. First Thessalonians 5:18 tells us to *give thanks in all circumstances*. That does not mean that you thank God *for* the terrible circumstances. As I pointed out before, we live in a fallen world, marred by sin, where bad things happen to good people. But *in* all things we can thank Him for who He is and for His unshakable truths: that we have been saved from sin and death, that we have been born again, that we have an eternal destiny, that we have a future and a hope, that we were once captives, and now we are free.

Cultivate a grateful heart. The word *cultivate* implies some effort! In our sinful natures, we are an ungrateful lot. We so often focus on our lack, our disappointment, our hurts. In so doing, how often do we miss the blessings God is trying to give us? So instead of focusing on your problems, dwell on the blessings God has sown in your day, evidence of His undying love for you: a concerned call from a friend, unexpected provision, an encouraging scripture, praise from a coworker. Instead of rehearsing to yourself—or anyone else who will listen—your troubles, think on the good things in your life.

As you grow in the Lord, you will come to thank Him *for* all things. Not for the cancer or the divorce or the alcoholism, but for His promise that what the devil intended for harm, the Lord means for good. *And we know that in all things God works for the good of those who love him, who have been called according to his purpose* (Romans 8:28).

5. Testify of the goodness of God

If we're honest, we have to admit that one of the first things we do when the storm hits is to make promises to God. "I promise, God, if only You will get me out of this, I'll never do that again." "I promise, God, if only You'll bring her back, I'll never act so selfishly again." "I promise, God, I'll never spend money like that again, if only You'll…"

But this is more wrong thinking! You do not have to appease God—as if He were an angry schoolmaster—with a promise of better behavior. He has already seen what you'll do, and He loves you anyway. God saw how I responded in that two-year time of crisis, and He loved, and continues to love, me anyway.

Instead of making promises to God, *declare God's promises to yourself.* In the midst of my own storm I began to declare:

"I have the mind of Christ."

"My mind has been renewed by the washing of the water of the Word."

"I have a future and a hope."

"My God will supply all my need."

Declaring these promises did not make my storm disappear, but rather reminded me of who our God is and who I am *in* Him. These positive declarations reminded me of His unfailing redemptive love and gave me faith and strength to get to the other side of my storm.

In his book, *God's Special Promises to Me*, Clift Richards writes,

One reason for much of the worry, stress, strain, and anxiety in our lives comes from failing to believe, remember, heed, or lay our claim to the promises of God...When we hear God's Word, He expects us to do it—to obey it, and to claim His promises even when the times are tough. He wants us to trust Him both in the good times and in the tough times. God's promises strengthen us and enable us to stand when the storms of life assail. It is at such times that the admonition of Ephesians encourages us..."that you may be able to withstand in the evil day, and having done all, to stand" (Ephesians 6:13 NKJV).[4]

KEY PROMISES FOR GOING THROUGH THE STORM

Here are just a few of God's many promises that will be of particular comfort when you are in the midst of a storm. Meditate on them, read them out loud, and memorize them!

"As I was with Moses, so I will be with you; I will never leave you nor forsake you. Be strong and courageous."

—Joshua 1:5-6

"God opposes the proud but gives grace to the humble." Submit yourselves, then, to God. Resist the devil, and he will flee from you. Come near to God and he will come near to you.

—James 4:6-8

The LORD is good, a refuge in times of trouble. He cares for those who trust in him.

—Nahum 1:7

The righteous cry out, and the LORD hears them; he delivers them from all their troubles. The LORD is close to the brokenhearted and saves those who are crushed in spirit. A righteous man may have many troubles, but the LORD delivers him from them all.

—Psalm 34:17-19

"So do not fear, for I am with you; do not be dismayed, for I am your God. I will strengthen you and help you; I will uphold you with My righteous right hand."

—Isaiah 41:10

"The LORD will guide you continually, and satisfy your soul in drought, and strengthen your bones; you shall be like a watered garden, and like a spring of water, whose waters do not fail."

—Isaiah 58:11 NKJV

Therefore he is able to save to the uttermost those who come to God through Him, since He always lives to make intercession for them.

—Hebrews 7:25 NKJV

I can do everything through [Christ] *who gives me strength.*

—Philippians 4:13

We know that in all things God works for the good of those who love him, who have been called according to his purpose.

—Romans 8:28

God…is able to do far more than we would ever dare to ask or even dream of—infinitely beyond our highest prayers, desires, thoughts, or hopes.

—Ephesians 3:20 TLB

CONCENTRATE ON WHAT GOD HAS DONE

One of the problems with storms is that they often reveal to us who we are and what is in us. We rarely measure up, even to our standards, do we? But God is not measuring us by our behavior or by our promises to do better. He wants us to stop looking at ourselves and look at Him. Stop looking at what you have done and look at what He has done. He loves us so much that He gave us His Son. He sent His Son *while we were still sinners.*

Declaring to yourself, then, the promises of God, His unchanging character, and His undying love will begin to turn your mind and heart towards the One who can and will sustain you and help you. And it will begin to put in your mouth a word of testimony about the goodness of God. God wants you to be able to rise up and declare His Word in the midst of the greatest adversity—without shame. And when you do—when you start telling the story of the cross, rather than your own story—people's lives will be changed.

6. Deal honestly in all things

Lastly, be honest with God. This seems like such a simple point, but we so often put on our most pious faces in the midst of our greatest trials. Do you want to master your storm? Deal honestly with God. Tell Him the truth. He can take it! In fact, He wants to take it. He wants to take your hurt, your disappointment, and your confusions and redeem them.

Go to God and tell Him, "I know that You're not surprised by this." "You saw what I did." "You know why I'm in this situation." God is not shocked by your emotions. He is not going to scold you or cast you from His presence. He wants you to come to Him as you are.

I like what Rick Warren says in his book, *The Purpose Driven Life*:

Pour out your heart to God. Unload every emotion you're feeling. Job did this when he said, "I can't be quiet! I am angry and bitter. I have to speak!" He cried out when God seemed distant: "Oh, for the days when I was in my prime, when God's intimate friendship blessed my house." God can handle your doubt, anger, fear, grief, confusion and questions. Did you know that admitting your hopelessness to God can be a statement of faith? Trusting God but feeling despair at the same time, David wrote, "I believed, so I said, 'I am completely ruined.'" This sounds like a contradiction: I trust God, but I'm wiped out! David's frankness actually reveals deep faith: First, he believed in God. Second, he believed God would listen to his prayer. Third, he believed God would let him say what he felt and still would love him.[5]

In being honest with God, you may get angry. You may get mad at yourself or at the situation. You may get mad at Him. The Bible says be angry, but do not sin. There's nothing wrong with anger, as long as it does not produce sin in your life. In fact, anger sometimes is the very thing that produces positive change in our lives. "I'm so angry because I did that. I won't do it again."

If you aren't open with God—if you keep Him on the outside—this is when the storm moves inside. You're afraid to tell God you're angry, depressed, and crushed, so you begin slowly but inevitably moving away from Him. You push away the very source of your comfort and healing.

He longs to walk with you through your storm, so be honest with Him about everything, and He will come alongside you and the storm will stay on the outside of your life.

If you will put these basic principles into practice, you *will* master whatever storm you are facing. Your feet will be planted on the Rock, and not even a tornado can blow you off course.

In the next chapter, we will look at how you can continue to stay on course during the storm. Staying on course is important not only for your own life, but it is important for everyone who is watching you as you navigate through your storm. Set a good example— others may be setting their courses by observing your actions and attitude.

Be on your guard; stand firm in the faith; be men of courage, be strong.

—1 Corinthians 16:13

And when they had preached the gospel to that city and made many disciples, they returned... strengthening the souls of the disciples, exhorting them to continue in the faith, and saying, "We must through many tribulations enter the kingdom of God."

—Acts 14:21-22 NKJV

In his heart a man plans his course, but the LORD determines his steps.

—Proverbs 16:9

CHAPTER TWO

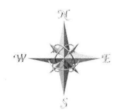

STAYING ON COURSE

OUR GREATEST ROLE MODEL, OF COURSE, IS our Lord Jesus. He faced many storms during His brief life on earth, but I want to focus on one in particular. At the very outset of His ministry, He faced the first storm, or what I call "opposition and opportunity." I think we all know what I mean by *opposition*, but by *opportunity*, I mean those occasions when we may be tempted to go the wrong way. The devil is always waiting for an "opportune time" to harass and discourage us and to throw us off course. But Jesus did not allow himself to be blown off course, to take a short cut, or to go a different way from the one God had marked out for Him. Let's look at how Jesus stayed the course in the face of the fiercest opposition a man has ever experienced:

Jesus, full of the Holy Spirit, returned from the Jordan and was led by the Spirit into the desert, where for forty days he was tempted by the devil. He ate nothing during those days, and at the end of them he was hungry. The devil said to him, "If you are the Son of God, tell this stone to become bread." Jesus answered, "It is written: 'Man does not live by bread alone.'"

The devil led him up to a high place and showed him in an instant all the kingdoms of the world. And he said to him, "I will give you all their authority and splendor, for it has been given to me, and I can give it to anyone I want to. So if you worship me, it will all be yours." Jesus answered, "It is written: 'Worship the Lord your God and serve him only.'"

The devil led him to Jerusalem and had him stand on the highest point of the temple. "If you are the Son of God," he said, "throw yourself down from here. For it is written: 'He will command his angels concerning you to guard you carefully; they will lift you up in their hands, so that you will not strike your foot against a stone.'" Jesus answered, "It says, 'Do not put the Lord your God to the test.'"

When the devil had finished all this tempting, he left him until an opportune time.

—Luke 4:1-13

At the beginning of Jesus' course, at the outset of His public ministry, the devil came to Him to tempt Him. It was a key moment in history. Jesus was beginning the countdown to your redemption and mine. Opposition and opportunity were presented to Him immediately.

FULL OF THE HOLY SPIRIT

But look at the key phrase that begins this passage: *Jesus, full of the Holy Spirit.* Jesus had just been baptized by John in the Jordan where He had received His Father's confirmation and affirmation: "*You are my Son, whom I love; with you I am well pleased*" (Mark 1:11). Immediately He was led by the Spirit into the desert where, *full of the Holy Spirit*, He resisted the devil. All the storms of this life, all the opposition and opportunity, cannot cause you to deviate from your destiny *if* you are full of the Holy Spirit.

As a boy, F. B. Meyer enjoyed visiting the Polytechnic, a science museum in London. One of the exhibits he liked most was a diving bell. It had no bottom, but there were seats attached to the rim at its base. At various times throughout the day, visitors were allowed to enter the diving bell and occupy those seats. It was then lowered into a deep tank of water. Meyer was fascinated by the fact that no water came up into the bell, even though its occupants could have reached out and dipped their fingers in the water. How was this possible? The bell did not fill with water because air was constantly being pumped into the bell from above. If a vacuum had existed, the water would have rushed in. Meyer then made this application to believers: "If you are full of the Holy Ghost, the flesh-life is underneath you, and though it would surge up, it is kept out."

DON'T ALTER YOUR COURSE

Let's look at the nature of Satan's temptations. Every one of the devil's temptations was designed to get Jesus to alter His course. First: *"tell this stone to become bread."* Jesus had not eaten for forty days. Of course He was hungry. The devil was tempting Him through the flesh. But his purpose was to get Jesus to change His course. Jesus had miracles in Him. Jesus could have turned the stone into bread. But it was not time. Furthermore, Jesus did not need to demonstrate His divinity to the devil: *"**If** you are the Son of God..."* He knew His identity, and He knew His destiny. He would not be blown off course.

The second temptation was the lust of the eyes. The devil offered Jesus all the *"authority and splendor"* of the kingdoms of this world if He would only worship him. Of course, the devil knew Jesus' destiny too. He knew that all authority and splendor ultimately belonged to Jesus, and that Jesus had come to restore that authority in us. But the devil desperately wanted Him to take a shortcut. "I will give you the world," he told Him. "You don't need to go to the cross for it." Jesus answered by telling him that He would worship God only and follow God's way.

We must follow Christ's example when the devil tempts us with an "easier" way. Our course in life does not permit us to go around mountains or over them—it calls for us to stand until the mountains are removed and cast into the sea. Maybe you think that your mountain isn't insurmountable—that with a few small decisions and some little compromises you can avoid having to go the route that God has laid out for you. But beware—it was only a "small" thing that Satan was tempting Jesus with; after all, the world already belonged to Jesus. Shouldn't it be His for the taking?

The prize oftentimes presents itself before the finish line in the form of the devil's temptations. Perhaps it seems far too costly to build your life according to Bible code—to take care of the "the details and small stuff." Maybe you think there's an easier way than "forgiving so you can be forgiven, bringing the 'whole' tithe into the storehouse, and blessing those who persecute you." But if we are to make it to the other side of our storms, we must trust God and obey His Word, our guidebook.

In his confrontation with Jesus, the devil knew what the prize would be for Jesus—and us—at the completion of Jesus' course. And Jesus knew that there could be no prize without a finish, so He stayed the course. We, too, must finish our course without compromising anywhere along the line.

Lastly, the devil took Jesus to the pinnacle of the temple and told Him to *throw himself down*. This was the temptation of the pride of life. The devil wanted Jesus to prove himself, and he also uses that trick on us. We often create our own storms by trying to prove to others who we are and what we are capable of doing. We want to prove our worth or value, which is a sign of our insecurity. But Jesus didn't have any insecurities. For Him to throw himself off the building would have been nothing but a publicity stunt, and He didn't need it. His publicity came through healing the sick, opening blind eyes, and raising the dead. It wasn't about Him—it was about them...and us. Jesus didn't come to "prove" himself—He came to seek and to save the lost.

A great storm of insecurity blew into my life when I began ministry. I was continually looking for the accolades of my family and the approval of my parents. I wanted to prove that I was called to preach, but I really wasn't very good, so I was actually asking people to lie about it. However, it wasn't long until I realized that ministry wasn't about me but about helping others… that it wasn't about obtaining the approval of others but about their healing…and mine. It was about getting on the other side of my storms—my storms of insecurity.

When Satan tells you to jump for the sake of proving yourself, don't do it. If you will stand strong in your storm of insecurity, your day will come, and it will be a day with purpose, not just a stunt. When you are looking for approval and applause to satisfy your soul, remember that it is simply pride, and choose instead to follow Jesus' example.

The devil was tempting Jesus to show that He had the authority given by God to save himself. But Jesus didn't come to save himself. He came to lose His life that He might save that which is lost. What the devil didn't realize was that Jesus didn't come to be thrown down; He came to be raised up. *By the Father. After the cross.* The devil wanted Jesus to alter His course, to deviate from His destiny. But *Jesus, full of the Holy Spirit*, resisted him, and the devil fled, waiting for another opportunity.

The flesh hungers for food, power, gratification, and so much more. Its appetite seems to never cease, so it must be disciplined. Jesus was hungry for food, and Satan, knowing the storm, offered to calm it by reminding Jesus that just by speaking the Word, He could turn a rock into bread. Satan also uses the hungers of the flesh and moments of crises to get us to alter our course today.

The greatest way to stay our course is by doing exactly what Jesus did to stay His—by living a life full of the Holy Spirit. The flesh will always wage war against God's will and His Spirit. Just try fasting for a day and see if your flesh doesn't scream for food. Even the leftovers that you didn't like yesterday look great to you today. Our flesh is strong but not as strong as the Holy Spirit. That's why the Bible tells us to *live by the Spirit, and you will not gratify the desires of the sinful nature* (Galatians 5:16).

The devil deals in counterfeits, lies, and temptations even in stormy marriages. If the storm in your marriage is raging and your physical relationship with your spouse is not good, the devil will try to convince you that another partner will fix the problem and calm your storm. But another person is not the answer to the craving of your flesh. A "counterfeit covenant" will not calm the storm of neglect and lack of intimacy. So don't fall for the devil's lies and temptation.

A person who is full of the Holy Spirit can spot temptation. The Holy Spirit reminds us of our purpose and path in life. We are aware of where we came from and where we are going, but we must not live in the past because our past is not the guide to our future. Our future looks radically different from our past. And if we are to follow God's plan for our future we must stay our course.

Jesus never lost sight of His goal. He knew the Father's plan, and He reminded himself, "I've got to stay my course in order to get people on their course." That was the will of God for Jesus, and that is the will of God for us as well. You and I must stay our course because other people are watching our course in order to set theirs.

There are three keys to staying on course, that I want to explain in depth.

KEEP YOUR HEAD

By "keeping your head," I do not mean primarily keeping your wits about you, although using your head to think clearly and make wise decisions certainly is important. I am using "head" in the biblical context of authority. "Head" or "headship" in the Bible refers to authority.

Paul writes about Jesus in Ephesians:

*God placed all things under his feet and appointed him to be **head** over everything for the church, which is his body, the fullness of him who fills everything in every way.*
> —Ephesians 1:22-23, emphasis added

Again, Paul writes about Jesus in Colossians:

*…he is the **head** of the body, the church; he is the beginning and the firstborn from among the dead, so that in everything he might have the supremacy.*
> —Colossians 1:18, emphasis added

Jesus said of himself, *"All authority in heaven and on earth has been given to me"* (Matthew 28:18). That authority, in other words, has been given or delegated to Him by the Father. On what basis has such supreme authority been given to Him? The answer is found throughout the New Testament, but perhaps nowhere more beautifully than in Philippians 2:

Who, being in very nature God, did not consider equality with God something to be grasped, but made himself nothing, taking the very nature of a servant, being made in human likeness. And being found in appearance as a man, he humbled himself and became obedient to death—even death on a cross! Therefore God exalted him to the highest place and gave him the name that is above every name, that at the name of Jesus every knee should bow, in heaven and on earth and under the earth, and every tongue confess that Jesus Christ is Lord, to the glory of God the Father.

—Philippians 2:6-11

Scripture tells us that because Jesus became obedient to death, God *raised him from the dead and seated him at his right hand in the heavenly realms, far above all rule and authority, power and dominion, and every title that can be given, not only in the present age but also in the one to come* (Ephesians 1:20-21).

No Authority without the Cross

Because Jesus stayed the course and submitted himself to His Father's plan, God gave Him supreme authority. Had Christ bowed to the devil's temptations, His authority would have been lost. There is no authority without the cross. There is no power without the cross.

But what do we make of Jesus' statement to His disciples (that includes you and me), *"I have given **you** authority...to overcome all the power of the enemy; nothing will harm you"* (Luke 10:19)? On what basis has Jesus given *us* such awesome authority?

Our Authority in Christ

From the moment we accept Christ's death for us on the cross, Scripture says we are justified before God. That means our sins have been forgiven, cancelled, forgotten. Moreover, we have been united with Christ! We have become one with Him.

In Galatians 2:20, Paul puts it this way, *I have been crucified with Christ and I no longer live, but Christ lives in me.* But not only have we been crucified with Him, we have also been buried, resurrected, and we have ascended with Him:

> *Because of his great love for us, God who is rich in mercy, made us alive with Christ… And God raised us up with Christ and seated us with him in the heavenly realms in Christ Jesus.*
>
> —Ephesians 2:4-6

We have authority because of what Christ did and because of the position we now have in Him. I like what Leo Harris says about our authority in Christ:

"What God says about you is true—you are born of God. A new creature in Christ, indwelt by Christ, and you can do all things through Christ! Your feelings may tell you that you are defeated, frustrated, struggling against overwhelming odds, but the WORD says you are more than a conqueror, a devil defeater, master in all circumstances, and standing on the threshold of unlimited possibilities—in Christ—and through faith in the WORD."[1]

Our Authority with God's Word

Because of that authority, Jesus says, *"...whatever you ask for in prayer, believe that you have received it, and it will be yours"* (Mark 11:24). The word *ask* here means "to require." You can speak to your mountain and tell it to be moved. You are not requiring something of God. You are requiring something of His Word, His promise.

Just recently I bought a computer desk for my youngest child, Victoria. I'm not the handiest guy around the house, but I told Victoria that I would assemble the desk for her. Weeks went by and I hadn't started the project. And on a regular basis, Victoria would come to me and, with a mother-like tone of voice, she would ask me, "Dad, when are you going to put my desk together?" She wasn't being disrespectful in asking; she was reminding me that I had given her my word that I would assemble her desk.

If I say to my children, "I am going to do thus and such for you," and they come back to me and simply ask me when I am going to do it, they're not requiring it of me. They are requiring it of my word. I told them this is what I would do, and they can count on my promise to do it.

God has said to us, "I am sending you My Word, My Covenant, My Testament, and I am telling you what I will do. So when you seek Me, you have authority to require of that Word what I will do."

We know that God doesn't forget, but He loves to hear us remind Him of His Word and promises. In Isaiah 43:26, He says, *Put Me in remembrance; let us contend together; state your case, that you may be acquitted* (NKJV). *The Living Bible* says it this way: *Oh, remind me of this promise of forgiveness, for we must talk about your sins. Plead your case for my forgiving you.*

Religious people are uncomfortable relating to God in this way. And yet God wants us to relate to Him in such a way that we believe every one of His words is true.

Power in Submission

But just as with Christ, our power comes from our submission. Our lives must be submitted to God. There is no power when we don't take up our cross to follow Him— our cross of submission, cooperation, acknowledgement that we are dependent upon Him, and that we are His servants. God did not force Jesus to lay down His life. Jesus said, *"...I lay down my life—only to take it up again. No one takes it from me, but I lay it down of my own accord. I have authority to lay it down and authority to take it up again. This command I received from my Father"* (John 10:17-18). Just as with Jesus, our power comes from our voluntarily taking up the cross to follow Him wherever He leads us, even through storms we did not expect.

Remember, the devil would like you to go any other way than the way of the cross. The devil was trying to get Jesus to expedite His destiny and His authority. We must not let anyone convince us there is a faster way to get where we are going. "Just cut this corner on your tax return." "If you put down your coworker, you can get his job." Don't fall into the devil's trap.

Speak to Your Doubts

Don't spend time talking about your storms and doubts—speak to them. Jesus had to speak to the doubt the devil was trying to sow in Him in the wilderness. Jesus answered those doubts by declaring the truth of God's

Word and the rightness of God's way in the face of hunger and adversity. Jesus met those challenges to His faith head-on.

You too must answer your doubts head-on. When your mind is confused and assaulted by opinion and criticism, you must look to God and say, "There is no doubt in my mind that Jesus gave His life for me; He has a destiny for me, and He has promised to get me through this storm. I put my trust in You. I will stay my course."

When we are assailed by doubt, we must access the disciplines of our life—our words and behavior. *Do not give the devil a foothold*, the Word says in Ephesians 4:27. Do not give him one inch by entertaining those doubts. Answer them with Scripture. Stay on course. **Keep your head.**

KEEP YOUR HEART

The second key to staying on course in the midst of adversity is keeping your heart. If *head* represents authority, *heart* represents attitude. Proverbs 4:23 says, *Keep your heart with all diligence, for out of it spring the issues of life* (NKJV). We have to guard our hearts from demonic opportunity and opposition that seek to prevent us from getting where we're supposed to go, learning everything we're supposed to learn, and developing the character we're supposed to develop.

What does the Scripture mean exactly when it says from our hearts "spring the issues of life"? The heart usually is associated with our emotions, but the Bible refers to "heart" in this way too. We are told repeatedly, for example, *"Love the LORD your God with all your heart..."* (Deuteronomy 6:5). Likewise, emotions, like sorrow, are attributed to the heart, such as when Jesus speaks to His disciples at the Last Supper, *"Because I have said these things to you, sorrow has filled your heart"* (John 16:6 NKJV).

But as the *Holman Bible Dictionary* points out, the heart can also refer to our thought life, such as in this proverb, *As he thinketh in his heart, so is he* (Proverbs 23:7 KJV).[2] The heart is also often referred to as the seat of our moral life. Jeremiah 17:10 says, *"I the Lord search the heart...to reward a man according to his conduct..."* Earlier in that same chapter of Jeremiah, the Lord says, *"The heart is deceitful above all things and beyond cure"* (Jeremiah 17:9).

Numerous additional references to the heart could also be cited, but suffice it to say that the Bible sees the heart as the center of the human personality. We must guard our hearts to keep our emotions, our thoughts, and our wills in line with God, so that we can stay the course in the midst of whatever adversity we encounter. We must not give bitterness, grumbling, or discouragement any place in our hearts, or we may give place to the devil who is constantly waiting for "an opportune time."

Jesus did not lose heart in the wilderness. He guarded His heart against the devil's temptations by affirming the truth of God's Word. And He did so with a good attitude. He didn't feel sorry for himself or complain to God: "Father, I'm suffering. Why didn't You tell me I'd be out here so long without food or water...and that the devil would constantly harass me?" No, Jesus knew He was in the will of God; therefore, He did not lose heart.

Change of Heart

Sometimes, to keep from losing heart, we need a change of heart. You and I have to recognize the authority of God. Whenever we are confronted by opposition and opportunity, there has to be a change of heart in order to overcome the challenge of our flesh.

This is often the greatest challenge we face when going through the storms of life. Satan has no greater weapon than to plant seeds of bitterness and resentment in our wounded hearts that will eventually cause our hearts to harden and become diseased. Heart disease never happens overnight; neither does the hardening of our spiritual hearts happen in a single moment or from a single trauma. It is a process over time, seed by seed, plaque by plaque, until our hearts become hardened, and we can no longer be used by God. God said, *"I will remove from you your heart of stone and give you a heart of flesh"* (Ezekiel 36:26). Hearts of flesh can receive the impression of Christ, but only if our hearts are tender is He able to imprint His heart on ours.

The writer of Hebrews warns us, quoting Psalm 95.

*"Today, if you hear his voice, **do not harden your hearts** as you did in the rebellion, during the time of testing in the desert... That is why I was angry with that generation, and I said, 'Their hearts are*

*always going astray…' So I declared on oath in my
anger, 'They shall never enter my rest.'"*
—Hebrews 3:7-8,10-11, emphasis added

The Ten Commandments were written on stone;
man could not keep them. The writer of Hebrews
reminds us that we have a new covenant, one written on
our hearts. *"The time is coming, declares the LORD, when
I will make a new covenant with the house of Israel… I
will put my laws in their minds and write them on their
hearts"* (Hebrews 8: 8, 10).

Watch out for symptoms of a hard heart: "I love God;
it's people I don't like." "I worship you, Jesus, but I really
can't forgive my husband for what he did." "I like my
job, but my boss is a fool." We don't think we have a
hard heart if we show up at church and volunteer, but
sometimes, carelessly, we let our hearts grow calloused.
Thus, a change is necessary. Instead, the Word says, *Show
that you are a letter from Christ…written not with ink but
with the Spirit of the living God, not on tablets of stone, but
on tablets of human hearts* (2 Corinthians 3:3). **We must
keep our hearts.**

KEEP YOUR HOPE (FAITH)

Faith represents anticipation or hope. Without confident anticipation, we lose heart, we lose faith, and we lose our heads. What is the basis for this anticipation? Why should we hope? Two things: first, what God has done for us in Christ—our salvation, our redemption, and our eternal destiny—and secondly, that *all the promises of God in Him are Yes, and in Him Amen...* (2 Corinthians 1:20 NKJV). We can count on the fulfillment of God's precious promises in our lives.

Christian hope has been explained like this:

Given the assurance of hope, Christians live in the present with confidence and face the future with courage. They can also meet trials triumphantly because they know that suffering produces perseverance; perseverance, character; and character, hope (Romans 5:3-4 NIV). Such perseverance is not passive resignation; it is the confident endurance in the face of opposition.[3]

Faith Must Be Exercised

You may have heard it said that faith is like a muscle; it must be exercised in order to become stronger. So *keeping* the faith conveys the idea of the active exercising of faith. As the above quote says, Christians are not "passively resigned" to circumstances. We exercise our faith in the confident expectation of God's provision and guidance and care.

A great example of exercising faith occurred when one of the most powerful storms ever recorded in earth's history hit Asia. Simply known now as the Tsunami, the storm swept across many countries in Asia, wiping out whole communities and devastating everything in its path. The calm waters of safety turned into a wave of death in a matter of minutes. With no time for preparation, many never knew what hit them.

When Daylan Sanders looked out from his small beachside orphanage in Sri Lanka, he saw a 30-foot wave towering over him and racing toward the shore. Within seconds he rounded up his wife and daughter, along with the 28 children in the orphanage, and raced toward the small 15-foot boat on the shoreline. As the children were piling into the small boat, Sanders looked out at the wave, held up his hand, and exercised his faith. Sanders said, "I command you, in the name of Jesus, to stop!" The tower of water that was sure to be their demise, slowed down. Sanders pointed the boat toward the wave and headed straight toward it. They were taking head-on the storm that was threatening to crush them.

I am not an experienced sailor, but I know that to take on a wave you must head your boat into it to avoid capsizing. As Sanders exercised his faith in the face of that devastating tsunami, his boat rode the wave and none were lost. We, too, must stand up in the midst of whatever is threatening us and exercise our faith, knowing that we have a powerful advocate in Jesus Christ.

God does not always want us to be dependent, like very young children, on the faith of others. Yes, there are times, as I said in the first chapter, when we reach out to others to strengthen our faith. Jennifer and I are deeply grateful for the prayers of our church. We appreciate their exercise of faith towards us, praying that our faith would not fail and that we would live the lives God has called us to. But while it is a precious privilege to pray for one another, God still wants us to exercise our own faith.

When our youngest child headed to camp for the first time, the first thing I did was check the weather reports. Thunderstorms were predicted for the first two days of camp, and my daughter hates thunderstorms! She has been afraid of them ever since she was a baby. She does her best in the midst of these storms, but when she's home, by about 3:00 a.m., she starts looking to our faith as she climbs into our bed. At those times, her actions are saying, "I'm depending on your faith, Mommy and Daddy, because in my room there ain't no faith going on right now!"

Sure enough, thunderstorms rolled in her second night at camp, and all the lights went out. We asked her later how she handled that. She told us that when one of her friends began crying, she went to comfort her. She assured her that everything would be all right. Mommy and Daddy were not there, so she had to exercise her own faith.

Jesus kept His faith when the devil tried to make Him alter His course and by-pass the way of the cross.

Jesus anticipated that if He did not throw himself down from the pinnacle of the temple, when He was crucified, God himself would raise Him up. If you will not throw yourself down when the devil says, "Be cast down!" you will not submit yourself to sin and evil. You will not be thrown off course. And just when you think your cross is about to crush you, God himself will raise you up.

You must exercise your faith because there will always be opposition and opportunity. In the midst of that opposition, keep the faith, stay the course, and watch how God answers your faith.

A woman in our church shared a wonderful story that illustrates how God can move when we keep the faith. This woman was told by her employer, "You will never go farther than you are right now. You have no education, no experience, and no credentials that would cause us to want to promote you." At first she was devastated. She thought her only recourse was to quit. But she kept her head. She went to God and asked Him what she should do. His answer was to stay right where she was. She decided this was an opportunity to trust God. "I'm not going to lose my head, my heart, or my faith—I will stay my course." In the last five years, she has been promoted five times, traveled the world, and her income has increased substantially as well.

The Word says that we must ...*contend for the faith*... (Jude 3). This implies that sometimes we must struggle to exercise it against opposition. God does not always remove the opposition. He wants us to exercise our faith, our courage, and our authority against that opposition. All opposition is not bad. Although God does not cause it, He uses it to strengthen us and to build character in us. The devil intends it for harm, but the Lord uses it for our good. ***We must keep our hope.***

When the storms of life assail, keep your head, keep your heart, and keep your hope. The Lord knows exactly where you are and where you are going. Stay on His course, and He will bring you through. He is the Master of your storm. He will never leave you nor forsake you. He is your deliverer, and the hand of providence will keep you.

There is nothing quite as potent as a focused life, one lived on purpose. The men and women who have made the greatest difference in history were the most focused.

—Rick Warren[1]

Grand Christian movements will rise and fall. Grand campaigns will be mounted and grand coalitions assembled. But all together such coordinated efforts will never match the influence of untold numbers of followers of Christ living out their callings faithfully across the vastness and complexity of modern society.

—Os Guinness[2]

CHAPTER THREE

GETTING TO THE OTHER SIDE

IN CHAPTER 2, WE LOOKED AT THE DANGERS OF not staying the course in our efforts to get to the other side of our storms. We learned the importance of not allowing adversity or temptation to deter (or detour) us or lure us into taking a shortcut. On the other side of whatever storm you are going through, people are waiting for what you are bringing to them. They may not know it yet, but God knows. Divine appointments have already been made for you on the other side.

You may not feel like you are bringing anything. Maybe you feel like you're just hanging on by your fingernails. But if you are following God—trying to keep your head, your heart, and your hope in Him— He is forging something in you that will help build His kingdom and help those in need.

DON'T COUNT YOURSELF OUT

Sometimes our biggest challenge in getting to the other side of our storms is not the circumstances or difficulties we're in but the choices we are making. The options are very simple: we can choose to blame others for the position we're in, or we can take charge of our lives and submit them to God, saying, "My situation doesn't matter, but my choices do. My decision is what matters today. And with God's help, I'm going to make right decisions and choices because I *am* going to the other side."

Some of us fall away or give up because of our past track records. We measure our future by our past. We're like that man whose friend asked him, "Why do you look so depressed? What are you thinking about?"

The man answered, "My future."

"Well, why does that seem so hopeless?" the friend persisted.

"Because of my past," the man replied.

Are you predetermining what you can do today based on what you did yesterday? Rick Warren has a great response to that: "We may be products of our past, but we're not prisoners of it. God's purpose is not limited by our past. He turned a murderer named Moses into a leader and a coward named Gideon into a courageous leader."[3]

The Scripture says this: *...forgetting what is behind and straining toward what is ahead, I press on toward the goal to win the prize for which God has called me heavenward in Christ Jesus* (Philippians 3:13-14).

So before we go one step further, let's clear up this matter of your past. God is not waiting until you're perfect to use you. He is not waiting till your dysfunctional family gets functional. We all have dysfunctional tendencies due to the sin nature, but God is ready to help us be overcomers. He is bringing you through to the other side of whatever trial you're facing because He intends to use you. He is building something in you that others desperately need.

FOLLOWING JESUS TO THE OTHER SIDE

Let's look at a well-known passage from Matthew to see what Jesus himself says about going to the other side. Jesus had just healed all the sick people who had been brought to Him, and He had driven out the spirits of "many who were demon-possessed." He had done what He intended to do, and it was time to move on.

> *When Jesus saw the crowd around him, he gave orders to cross to the other side of the lake. Then a teacher of the law came to him and said, "Teacher, I will follow you wherever you go."*
>
> *Jesus replied, "Foxes have holes and birds of the air have nests, but the Son of Man has no place to lay his head."*
>
> *Another disciple said to him, "Lord, first let me go and bury my father."*
>
> *But Jesus told him, "Follow me, and let the dead bury their own dead."*
>
> *Then he got into the boat and his disciples followed him. Without warning, a furious storm came up on the lake, so that the waves swept over the boat. But Jesus was sleeping. The disciples went*

and woke him, saying, "Lord, save us! We're going to drown!"

He replied, "You of little faith, why are you so afraid?" Then he got up and rebuked the winds and the waves, and it was completely calm.

The men were amazed and asked, "What kind of man is this? Even the winds and the waves obey him!"

When he arrived at the other side in the region of the Gadarenes, two demon-possessed men coming from the tombs met him. They were so violent that no one could pass that way.

—Matthew 8:18-28

Jesus had stern words here for two would-be disciples. When the first man boldly said, "I will follow You wherever You go," Jesus informed him that following the Son of Man would not be easy. Then he reminded him that even the birds and the animals have homes, but He does not. Jesus wanted the man to understand that following Him would require sacrifice, especially the sacrifice of self, and that following Him would, from time to time, bring trials of many kinds.

To the other disciple who first wanted to go and bury his father, Jesus answered more sternly, *"Follow me, and let the dead bury their own dead."* This verse troubles many people, and certainly it was scandalous in Jesus' own time. Jewish law and custom held the honoring of mother and father as the highest importance, especially the duty of burying a parent. However, Jesus was not being insensitive here. Many theologians believe that this disciple's father was not yet dead. What he was really saying to Jesus was, "Can't I wait until my father dies? Then I will follow You." In other words, "Can't I wait until all the natural things line up in my life, and then do the supernatural?" Jesus' response was, "You're waiting on death instead of following life. Now is the time to follow Me to the other side."

Jesus warns all who would follow Him that the journey requires wholehearted commitment, and He tells us to count the cost, and then to follow Him without ever looking back.

JESUS KNOWS ABOUT OUR STORMS IN ADVANCE

The passage from Matthew 8:23-24 says that Jesus *got in the boat and his disciples followed him. Without warning, a furious storm came up on the lake, so that the waves swept over the boat. But Jesus was sleeping.* Luke 8:23 says, *A squall came down on the lake, so that the boat was being swamped, and they were in great danger.* Jesus knew the storm was coming. It didn't surprise Him; that's why He slept. Even though the waves broke over the boat, so that it was nearly swamped, Jesus slept. *Jesus was at rest.*

Remember that the disciples with Jesus were fishermen. They were used to the sudden, violent squalls that occur on the Sea of Galilee. This storm must have been unusually severe, because the Bible says they feared for their lives. They awakened Jesus, and first He rebuked the storm; then He rebuked the disciples for their lack of faith.

What was really going on? Jesus got the disciples into the boat for a specific reason. "Let's go over to the other side," He told them. He wanted to show them that in order to get to the other side, sometimes they would have to pass through storms that were beyond anything they had ever encountered. "Have faith in Me," He told them. "You can get through this. I will not always be with you physically, but you can still trust Me to bring you through."

The other reason Jesus got them in that boat was to show them that there were needs on the other side of the storm that were bigger than they were, and He wanted them to understand that it was not about them at all. Waiting on the other side were two tortured, demon-possessed men whom Jesus, of course, set free.

You see, on the other side of the storms of your life, it's not just about you. It's not just about me. When I'm going through a storm, I have come to recognize that there are other people waiting to see how I get through my storm. There are people waiting on the other side of my storm who need faith, the faith I am bringing in my boat. There are other people waiting for you and for me.

THE KEY TO LIFE IS FOCUS = *hunger & thirsting*

In order to stay the course and get to the other side, we must be driven by purpose. Purpose will keep you focused. If I were to ask you right now, "What is your focus in life?" many of you might answer, "I've got to be at work tomorrow at 7:30 or 8:30." I'm focused on working for the purpose of making money. If I asked you, "What are you going to do when you get home Monday night or Tuesday night, or later in the week?"

many people would not be able to articulate their plan. Too often we are being carried along by circumstance, by time, by obligations. Obviously, we need to earn a living and support our families, but what is our real purpose? We have to have a purpose or a focus that will drive us to the other side.

CURIOSITY CREATES FOCUS

What creates that focus? Curiosity is the number-one tool in creating focus. The Bible is full of examples of people first being drawn to God by curiosity. Perhaps the best example is Moses who went over to investigate a burning bush that was not consumed. It was curiosity that drew Moses to that bush where he heard the voice of God and where he was called to lead the nation of Israel out of bondage. Many people first went to hear Jesus out of curiosity.

One of the problems with most adults today is that we have lost our sense of curiosity! Certainly, this must be partly what Jesus meant when He said we must become like little children. Children are curious; they want to see how things work; they want to explore and investigate and ask lots of questions.

When I was born again in 1977, and was thus just a little child in the Lord, I was curious about all the things of God. I was curious about miracles and all the things I had always heard preached against. I had grown up in a strict church that had a clouded understanding of miracles, signs, and wonders. But after I was born again, I wanted to find out for myself about all of these things.

Not long after I met the Lord, I also met Jennifer, the woman who would become my wife. I didn't yet know much about her. She told me that she grew up in a Methodist church, which I thought sounded pretty safe! So I asked her one day if she would go with me to the Civic Center to hear Kenneth Hagin preach. After listening for hours, I couldn't find anything wrong with the worship or the message. I asked Jennifer if there was anything wrong with what we had just heard, and of course, she said no. It turns out that she was an undercover charismatic! She was just waiting for me to submit myself to believing that signs and wonders and the gifts of the Spirit are for today.

For the twelve years we have been in this community, I have prayed that God would give the people driving by a holy curiosity about our church. Of course, when you have a building as ugly as our original building was—it looked like a crack house—you probably would be curious about why so many cars were in the parking lot. Many of the members of our church are here because of their initial curiosity. As a result, families have been saved and marriages have been restored.

Don't ever grow so old that you're not curious about the things of God. Curiosity will drive you to prayer, drive you to reading your Bible, and drive you to church! When I'm on vacation, I hate missing church because I am curious to see what God is going to do while I'm gone.

Be curious about what is ahead—what awaits you on the other side is a God-appointed adventure.

HAVE A CAUSE *Key to hunger + thirsting*

If you want to stay focused, have a cause. Most immature Christians think, *I will die for a cause*, but mature Christians understand that we are called to *live* for a cause. Causes take the selfishness out of us; they create a selfless individual who wants to do something for God.

Let's return to our example of Moses. In his book *The Vision*, Gerald Coates writes this:

Almost every major biblical figure who served God had a vision. Moses not only received instructions (the Law), but a vision. It was during his encounter [at the burning bush] that he was given a clear vision and instructions as to how to fulfil that vision. That call, to cooperate with God "to deliver the Israelites from the power of the Egyptians, and to bring them up from that land to a good and spacious land," filled his heart and mind for another forty years. In times of darkness, depression, squabbling and defeat, it was that call and vision that kept him on course.[4]

Coates points to other men of vision like Joshua, Paul, and Peter: their vision gave them a cause outside of themselves that allowed them not only to endure countless storms, but to profoundly influence countless generations. Of course, the supreme example of living a life of vision is the Lord Jesus: "He was not only to bring forgiveness of sin, but he was to implant a new spirit, a visionary spirit, the Holy Spirit, to every repentant wrongdoer."[5]

Where there is no vision, the people perish (Proverbs 29:18 KJV). Is this why so many people die shortly after they retire? I first noticed this phenomenon in my twenties. I would hear of a friend of the family retiring, and several months later my mother would announce they were going to that person's funeral. For years this individual had a cause. After he retired, this gifted man lost his focus. I like Winston Churchill's retort to a friend who remarked that "there was something to be said for being a *retired* Roman Emperor. 'Why retired?' Churchill growled. 'There's nothing to be said for *retiring* from anything.'"[6]

Friends, I am not against retirement! But find a new purpose or cause that will energize your life and propel you outside of yourself into the hurting world.

HAVE A CALLING

It is important to find your calling. First, let's remember that all Christians share one fundamental calling. We have been *called* by God, and our *calling* is to respond with absolute love and devotion to Him. Os Guinness puts it like this: "We are not primarily called to do something or go somewhere; we are called to Someone. We are not called first to special work but to God."[7]

All of us are called to love God with all of our heart, soul, mind, and strength. This is our first and foremost calling. But God has also gifted each of us to fulfill His various purposes in the world. Our individual callings follow these gifts. Guinness calls this our "secondary calling," our calling to motherhood, or business, or politics, or teaching, or wherever our talents and abilities lead. But again, your calling, your gifts are not just for yourself. "Our gifts are ultimately God's, and we are only stewards—responsible for the prudent management of property that is not our own."[8]

Dorothy Sayers, one of the Inklings, that group of Christian writers which included C. S. Lewis and J. R. R. Tolkien, wrote a great deal on the subject of work and vocation. "[Work] should be looked upon—not as a necessary drudgery to be undergone for the purpose of making money, but as a way of life in which the nature of man should find its proper exercise and delight and so fulfil itself to the glory of God."[9] Work, she says, "should be the thing in which [man] finds spiritual, mental, and bodily satisfaction, and the medium in which he offers himself to God."[10]

God will use the work we perform for Him—done with all our hearts—to give us satisfaction, yes, but also to build His kingdom.

If I had fully understood this in my job twenty-five years ago with the telephone company, I would have been climbing telephone poles for Jesus! The call on your life will keep you motivated and focused. Jesus had a vision and a call, and because of them He went to the other side, *through the storms*. He knew the Gadarenes were waiting. This is what I call "postage stamp Christianity." Consider the postage stamp. Its usefulness consists in its ability to stick to one thing till it gets there. So continue to walk in your calling and gifts. They will help you stay focused even in the midst of opposition and adversity.

It will always lead to opportunity!

BE FLEXIBLE

Don't become so focused, however, that you become inflexible. Flexibility is key to mastering your storm. Sometimes we become so driven that we become dogmatic about how things must be done. But if you can't bend before the winds, you will break. Flexible people let other people be right. Flexible people also take time for those around them, like Jesus did with the disciples in the boat. He didn't have to get into the boat with them. He could have translated himself to the other side. But He wanted to go with the disciples; there were things to be shared and learned. He didn't lose sight of His goal, nor did He forget those who were with Him.

In the early years of pastoring Victory, I still did a lot of administrative duties. One day I went to a daycare auction because the church needed some childcare equipment. Other business owners were there because other equipment and furniture was also being sold. I began talking to one of them, and eventually invited him to come to church. I could tell he wanted to shock me, so he said, "Can I bring my margarita?" "Sure," I replied without missing a beat. "We have a margarita section!"

God loves people. If we want to reach the Gadarenes of our day, we need to be flexible.

SIGNS OF FLEXIBILITY

Let me give you a sure sign of flexibility: a sense of humor. Can you laugh at yourself? When you make a mistake, can you laugh, or do you always have to be right? Recently I was in Las Vegas, preaching at Victory Vegas Church. When I got on the airplane to come home, I chose, as I always do, to sit in the exit row seat—row 27F. I decided long ago that "in the event of a water landing," I wanted to be the one to open the door. A man began moving down the aisle towards me, with a very recognizable look on his face. I fly all the time, so I know all the "airline looks." This was a "you're in my seat" look. I could see that he didn't want to appear to be mad, so he made an effort to say somewhat politely, "We have a mistake here. You're in my seat. My seat is 27D."

"No, sir," I replied pointing to the seat next to me. That's 27D."

The man looked shocked, and he actually said, "You know, I'm never wrong."

"Well," I said, "if that's a problem, I can help you, because I'm wrong regularly." The guy next to me lost it! So, if you need "wrong" counseling you can come to me!

A few years ago I probably would not have handled the situation quite like that. I would have been far more tempted to say, "Sit down and shut up! Can't you read?" But I have a sense of humor now, and I understand that it's not always about being right.

Be open to new ideas. Project an attitude of inventiveness and creativity. These are all signs of flexibility. Speak and move with ease and spontaneity. Don't let crises and stress immobilize you. It's not that they won't affect you, but they don't have to immobilize you.

FINISH WELL

People who are pursuing their purpose and going to the other side are people who finish. Getting to the other side is not just a physical accomplishment. Physically you may have made it to church on Sunday. But some of you may have left your spirit at home. You're mad at your husband or your wife. You've brought with you the offense you took from another person. God wants your spirit, soul, and body on the other side.

Some of us also want to quit because we can't be first when we get there. I call this the "number one" problem, and it is a big problem in our culture. If I can't be the best, or number one, or boss, I quit. This mentality is straight from our fallen nature. But don't quit just because you're not the best, or the greatest, or the boss.

Jesus also is not looking for style points! He is looking for faithfulness, not perfection. He is looking for men and women who, no matter what they've been through, will press on to the other side. Some day He will put a medal around your neck and a crown upon your head.

I have been around some of the greatest pastors in America. There were times when I listened to what they were doing and thought, *Why do I exist? We're not even near to doing some of the things they are accomplishing.* But today it does not bother me at all. What matters is that you are in the race, and that you are going to finish. What matters is that you are obeying God.

Finishers are future-minded. They see beyond their present circumstance. They see beyond their generation. They are people who don't hold grudges and offenses. We can't get to the other side with an anchor of bitterness. When finishers show up, everything about them shows up—heart, mind, body, and soul. They refuse to be defeated. They refuse to let the storm keep them from their destiny. They face their storm, stay their course, and they get to the other side. How you begin your race matters, but how you finish it matters more. Stay the course and go on to the other side.

For our struggle is not against flesh and blood, but against the rulers, against the authorities, against the powers of this dark world and against the spiritual forces of evil in the heavenly realms.

—Ephesians 6:12

We are not ignorant of [Satan's] schemes.

—2 Corinthians 2:11 NASU

CHAPTER FOUR

SUPERNATURAL STORMS

ETTING TO THE OTHER SIDE OF YOUR STORM is not about merely surviving whatever trial you are facing. Getting to the other side is fundamentally about meeting the needs of the people you're going to find there. As we saw in the previous chapter, having this as your goal will help drive you to the other side; having a clear purpose outside of yourself—even at the time you are most tempted to be focused on self—will give you the determination you need to go through your storm prepared for the people God is bringing to you.

Jesus brought His disciples through the storm on the Sea of Galilee because He knew there were people who needed Him on the other side. But He also wanted to show His disciples how to handle a different kind of storm. He had just taught His disciples about natural storms; now He wanted to teach them about supernatural ones.

Let's pick up the story in Mark, chapter 5:

They went across the lake to the region of the Gerasenes. When Jesus got out of the boat, a man with an evil spirit came from the tombs to meet him. This man lived in the tombs, and no one could bind him any more, not even with a chain. For he had often been chained hand and foot, but he tore the chains apart and broke the irons on his feet. No one was strong enough to subdue him. Night and day among the tombs and in the hills he would cry out and cut himself with stones.

When he saw Jesus from a distance, he ran and fell on his knees in front of him. He shouted at the top of his voice, "What do you want with me, Jesus,

Son of the Most High God? Swear to God that you won't torture me!" For Jesus had said to him, "Come out of this man, you evil spirit!" Then Jesus asked him, "What is your name?"

—Mark 5:1-9

This was a curious exchange. Jesus was not addressing the man who came out to meet Him. He addressed the spirit that was controlling that man. This is clear from the response: *"My name is Legion," he replied, "for we are many."* The spirit identified himself through the mouth of the man. *And he begged Jesus again and again not to send them out of the area* (Mark 5:9-10).

SUPERNATURAL STORMS

In the first chapter we looked at storms caused by difficult circumstances like financial problems, unemployment, illness, or death. These are storms caused by living in a fallen world. In this chapter I want us to look at a different kind of storm, a relational storm whose origin is in the supernatural realm.

It is so important that we understand this kind of storm. Some of us have looked at people we know, and we have made them out to be the problem. *They are not the problem.* The Word says, *For our struggle is not against flesh and blood, but against the rulers, against the authorities, against the powers of this dark world and against the spiritual forces of evil in the heavenly realms* (Ephesians 6:12). We are not warring against people, Paul says, but against the spirits of darkness who control or influence them.

DANGER OF IGNORANCE

Many believers do not understand that there are spirits that come to deceive, manipulate, and destroy us. Christians cannot be possessed by a demon because demons cannot live where the Spirit of God resides. But we can unwittingly battle oppressive spirits that can have a destructive influence in our lives and in our relationships with others. And the enemy of our soul is quite content with our ignorance about him.

In his book entitled *Know Your Real Enemy*, Michael Youssef describes our battle with spiritual forces as the "invisible war." He writes, "Tragically, when it comes to the invisible war, Christians are big on ignorance.

Probably not one in ten believers would identify Satan as the real Enemy, much less know how to fight him."[1]

Youssef goes on to say that "our spiritual being" is like a "house with many doors." Each door leads into our soul; thus, each door needs to be firmly locked against the one who *"comes only to steal and kill and destroy"* (John 10:10). There are many doors by which the enemy can enter—through unresolved anger, jealousy, greed, lust, the occult—but the first door by which he gains access, Youssef argues, is ignorance.[2]

So we must first acknowledge that we are in a battle, no less real and fierce than if we could see the opposing armies facing off on the field of combat. This battle, however, has one unique feature. This is one whose outcome is already known.[3]

We know that the ultimate victory was secured by Christ at the cross and the resurrection. *And having disarmed the powers and authorities, he made a public spectacle of them, triumphing over them by the cross* (Colossians 2:15). But we also know that until Jesus returns and Satan reaches his predicted end in the lake of fire, we will still do battle with him. Scripture is clear

about this when it warns, *Be self-controlled and alert.*
Your enemy the devil prowls around like a roaring lion
looking for someone to devour (1 Peter 5:8-9).

Eph. 6:10, 11-14

✳ KNOW YOUR ENEMY

Whether we acknowledge it or not, or like it or not,
we are in a battle with unseen and wicked forces. Our
first responsibility, as with anyone going into battle,
is to learn everything we can about our adversary. No
soldier goes into battle without gathering every bit of
intelligence he can about his enemy's tactics and strate-
gies. While it is not my purpose to do an in-depth study
here on this subject, I want to point out some information that is crucial to responding to the storms the evil
one stirs up in our relationships.

SATAN IS A CREATED BEING

First of all, we know that Satan was created by God.
He was chief among his angelic host until pride and
the desire to be God led him to spearhead a rebellion
in heaven. Some biblical scholars believe this passage in
Ezekiel describes Satan and his fall:

SUPERNATURAL STORMS

"You were the model of perfection, full of wisdom and perfect in beauty... You were anointed as a guardian cherub, for so I ordained you... You were blameless in your ways from the day you were created till wickedness was found in you... Your heart became proud on account of your beauty, and you corrupted your wisdom because of your splendor. So I threw you to the earth..."

—Ezekiel 28:12, 14, 15, 17

Isaiah describes Satan like this:

How you have fallen from heaven, O morning star, son of the dawn! You have been cast down to the earth... You said in your heart, "I will ascend to heaven; I will raise my throne above the stars of God..." But you are brought down to the grave, to the depths of the pit.

—Isaiah 14:12, 13-15

Jesus himself says in Luke 10:18, *"I saw Satan fall like lightning from heaven."*

SATAN'S CHIEF TACTIC

I delve into Satan's origins here for only two purposes: one, to remind you that Satan is a created being. He was created by God. As a created being, he is not on an equal footing with God—his strength and power are not in any way equal to God's. This is not to say he is without power—that would be the opposite error of ignoring him altogether. But because he cannot fight God head-on and win, he uses a different tactic, and this is my second point. Satan's primary weapon against us is deception. Jesus calls him the "father of lies." *"He was a murderer from the beginning, not holding to the truth, for there is no truth in him. When he lies, he speaks his native language, for he is a liar and the father of lies"* (John 8: 44). In Revelation, he is called...*the great dragon...who leads the whole world astray.* The *New King James Version* says, he...*deceives the whole world...*(Revelation 12:9).

Isn't this our first picture of Satan's activities in the Garden with Eve? He doesn't intimidate, threaten, or overcome her—he sets out to deceive her by getting her to believe a lie about God. "Did God really say...?" He leads her to question and then doubt God's Word and, really, God's love. Once he planted that lie and she accepted it, disobedience and ruin followed.

Neil Anderson writes in *The Beginner's Guide to Spiritual Warfare:*

> Deception is a very clever and effective tactic, because if someone attacks you, you know it. You can defend yourself, whether the attack is verbal or physical.
>
> If someone tempts you, you know it. You have a choice to make. But if someone deceives you, you don't know it. If you knew it you wouldn't be deceived. You accept what is being told to you as the truth and proceed to act on it... Yes, deception is a very effective means of control. Actually Satan has to tell unbelievers only one lie to keep them under his control. That lie is that there is a way to find true life other than through the cross of Jesus Christ.[4]

We must begin with the fact, then, that unbelievers are already caught in a lie and are influenced and often controlled by Satan. *The god of this age has blinded the minds of unbelievers...* (2 Corinthians 4:4). This is not, of course, a cause for pride in us. Paul reminds us in Ephesians:

> *As for you, you were dead in your transgressions and sins, in which you used to live when you followed the ways of the world **and of the ruler of the kingdom of the air, the spirit who is now at work in those who are disobedient**. All of us also lived among them at one time, gratifying the cravings of our sinful nature and following its desires and thoughts... But because of his great love for us, God who is rich in mercy, made us alive with Christ even when we were dead in transgressions...*
>
> —Ephesians 2:1-4, emphasis added

We need to remember who is really pulling the strings of nonbelievers. Have you ever noticed that the people who need your help the most are often the most difficult to help? You must remember that you are not struggling with people, but with the spirit of the ruler of this world.

DON'T GIVE THE DEVIL A FOOTHOLD

Furthermore, the Bible tells us that we must be "self-controlled and alert" and not give the enemy a foothold. The basis of all spiritual warfare is a right relationship with God. "Spiritual warfare," Anderson argues, "is not just a question of technique—saying the right words, doing the right things, using the right objects, praying the right prayers... It is not a matter of technique but of relationship. Our relationship with our Lord is basic to understanding and dealing with our relationship with our enemy."[5]

A right relationship with God, one based on love, humility, submission, and a genuine desire to serve Him, will help us resist the enemy. It is not my purpose to get into a full-blown discussion of spiritual warfare, but I do want to emphasize one point, which is significant to the storms we inevitably encounter when we minister to nonbelievers. One of the reasons I have made such an issue of the true enemy behind our relational storms is to help us avoid picking up offense against those individuals. Of course, we can easily be offended by believers as well—perhaps more deeply offended because our expectations are higher—but the fruit of hanging on to hurts is equally devastating.

DON'T HANG ON TO OFFENSE

In his excellent book, *The Bait of Satan*, John Bevere notes that in relationships "the possibilities for offense are as endless as the list of relationships"—in fact, of course, the hurt and injury is greater the closer that person is to us.[6] Sometimes, we have been genuinely mistreated—we have been lied to, cheated on, falsely accused, etc.; other times we *think* we have been wronged. In either case, though, Bevere says, the results of hanging on to the offense are "insults, attacks, wounding, division, separation, broken relationships, betrayal, and backsliding."[7]

As a result of feeling offended, we can become angry, resentful, bitter, or hard-hearted. But Psalm 119:165 says, *Great peace have they which love thy law: and nothing shall offend them* (KJV).

It is in the context of unresolved anger that we are admonished in Ephesians, *In your anger do not sin. Do not let the sun go down while you are still angry, and do not give the devil a foothold* (Ephesians 4:26-27). We must be vigilant, therefore, to search our hearts and forgive every offense against us and release every offender. Paul exhorts us to *let all bitterness, wrath, anger, clamor, and evil speaking be put away from you, with all malice. And be kind to one another, tenderhearted, **forgiving one another, even as God in Christ also forgave you*** (Ephesians 4:31-32 NKJV, emphasis added).

We have been entrusted by God with "the ministry of reconciliation":

> *So from now on we regard no one from a worldly point of view. Though we once regarded Christ in this way, we do so no longer. Therefore, if anyone is in Christ, he is a new creation; the old has gone, the new has come! All this is from God, who reconciled us to himself through Christ and gave us the ministry of reconciliation: that God was reconciling the world to himself in Christ, not counting men's sins against them. And he has committed to us the message of reconciliation. We are therefore Christ's ambassadors, as though God were making his appeal through us.*

> —2 Corinthians 5:16-20

PIG MENTALITY

Let's return to Jesus and the Gerasene demoniac. I want to highlight another kind of relational storm—the one that's often unleashed in a community (or family) in response to our helping someone else.

> *A large herd of pigs was feeding on the nearby hillside. The demons begged Jesus, "Send us among the pigs; allow us to go into them." He gave them permission, and the evil spirits came out and went into the pigs. The herd, about two thousand in number, rushed down the steep bank into the lake and were drowned.*
>
> *Those tending the pigs ran off and reported this in the town and countryside, and the people went out to see what had happened. When they came to Jesus, they saw the man who had been possessed by the legion of demons, sitting there, dressed and in his right mind; and they were afraid. Those who had seen it told the people what had happened to the demon-possessed man—and told about the pigs as well. Then the people began to plead with Jesus to leave their region.*
>
> —Mark 5:11-17

Earlier in this passage, we are given a poignant picture of this demon-possessed man. He had been completely isolated from society and was living in the "tombs," a place of death, rather than life. The spirit controlling him turned him into someone so terrifying that the townspeople had chained him "hand and foot." But with his supernatural strength, he broke the chains and wandered aimlessly among the tombs "crying out" and injuring himself.

We are not told how this man got into this condition, but we do know that Jesus was moved to help him. He compelled the spirits to come out of the man and allowed them to enter a nearby herd of pigs. Look at what happens next though, in response to the man's deliverance. When the townspeople came to see what had happened, they found the man, the one who had been tormenting their region, "dressed and in his right mind." Were they glad? Relieved? Awed? Thankful? No, the Word says, "they were afraid... [and] began to plead with Jesus to leave their region."

Isn't this strange? They didn't thank Jesus for freeing them from this terrifying man; they were more interested in what became of their pigs. Their focus was not on the deliverance but on their economic loss. This is what I call "pig mentality." By blinding our thinking, evil spirits create a mentality that cares more about things than people. Clearly, a major economic loss was suffered when a large herd like this was drowned. But the pig mentality has the perspective all wrong.

GETTING COMFORTABLE WITH EVIL SPIRITS

Let's examine more closely the pig part of the story because it sheds light on the townspeople's reaction. When the evil spirits possessing the man identified themselves as "Legion," they also begged Jesus not to "send them out of the area." The spirits in the man had become comfortable in that area, perhaps because the people were also comfortable with them. In other words, the people were no threat to the spirits. The spirits knew they were in control of that area, so they asked to stay there.

If we are not careful, like the people of that region, we, too, can become so comfortable with the spirits of our age, or our culture, that we are not alarmed by its growing godlessness and defiance towards God. We are not startled any longer when people want to remove

God from the Pledge of Allegiance or take His name off our currency. Does it really matter all that much? Yes, it really matters all that much! There is a spirit who wants to remove from our society the influence of the Most High God, the One who parts the seas, the One who hung the stars in the sky, the One who raises the dead, the One who procured your salvation and mine. We must never become comfortable with that spirit!

TERRITORIAL SPIRITS

Increasing attention has been paid in recent years to the idea of territorial spirits, that is, demons who "are assigned to geographical areas, cultural groups, nations, cities or 'countrysides.'"[8] Popular books like Frank Peretti's *This Present Darkness* focus our attention on the possibility that supernatural power struggles could have a far bigger influence on human events than anyone previously thought.

More scholarly writings, like those of C. Peter Wagner, have documented persuasive evidence that Satan indeed "delegates high ranking members of the hierarchy of evil spirits to control nations, regions, cities, tribes, people groups, neighborhoods, and other signifcant social networks of human beings throughout the world."[9] Intercessors around the world have discovered that identifying these demonic forces and breaking their strongholds through prayer causes remarkable breakthroughs in evangelism.

In our story of the Gerasene demoniac, we see a region that seems to be controlled by a territorial spirit of greed. So much so that the people living there would rather have their demoniac back than lose their precious pigs. They were afraid of the Holy Spirit who had broken into their area, but they were not even aware of their bondage to a very different kind of spirit. Jesus wanted His disciples—both then and now—to see that there is a supernatural war raging, and that our ministry to those in need will sometimes produce another kind of supernatural storm. Jesus simply met a need, and out of that came a storm.

Let's see how Jesus responded to this storm.

As Jesus was getting into the boat, the man who had been demon-possessed begged to go with him. Jesus did not let him, but said, "Go home to your family and tell them how much the Lord has done for you, and how he has had mercy on you." So the man went away and began to tell in the Decapolis how much Jesus had done for him. And all the people were amazed.

—Mark 5:18-20

What did Jesus do? He simply got back in the boat and left. He didn't hang around to explain what He did or defend himself. He didn't give an interview in the *Decapolis Times,* detailing the outstanding miracle He had just performed. He urged the delivered man to go and tell his friends and family the great thing God had done. But he left the people there to what they preferred, because on the other side of the lake, people were waiting who needed Him—Jairus and the woman with the issue of blood. Basically, Jesus was saying, "I have given you free will. You can have the Holy Spirit, or you can have these spirits."

You see, the spirits had not left. When the pigs drowned, the spirits didn't. They just needed a place to go temporarily. In Matthew 12:43, we are told that "*when a defiling evil spirit is expelled from someone, it drifts along through the desert looking for an oasis, some unsuspecting soul it can bedevil"* (THE MESSAGE). So Jesus left them to the spirits they had chosen.

This town was ungrateful. I don't believe Jesus would have allowed the legion of evil spirits to stay there if the people had been grateful, because gratitude is born of the Holy Spirit. The minute we get grateful, God says, "Now I can do something." Ingratitude is born of self-ishness, pride, and a desire to be in control. But we don't really have control, as I think we have now seen.

RESIST EVERY EVIL INFLUENCE

Be careful of the influences you allow in your lives. We must not be "ignorant of the enemy's devices." As a youth pastor, I was invited into homes where children were experiencing all kinds of trouble. When I walked into their bedrooms with their parents, all over their walls were posters of demonic bands. I told the parents that they had invited all kinds of evil influence into their home, and that they must rid themselves of every evil influence! So it is today—we must always be on guard against the evil influences that attempt to invade our lives every day.

SUPERNATURAL STORMS

The Holy Spirit comes to do you good—to empower you, bless you, and comfort you. He comes to guide you, restore you, and counsel you. That's who the Holy Spirit is. Evil spirits come to destroy. Those spirits will isolate you and separate you from the power and presence of God. They will deceive you into believing that you can't be healed or forgiven…that you are not worthy of God's love. You must reject this spirit and speak to it as Jesus did, telling it to come out of this situation. Say to the spirit, "You are the barrier between my mother and me. You are the barrier between my father and me… between my children and me. In the name of Jesus, I command this spirit of division to be gone."

Supernatural relational storms are inevitable because the enemy of our soul wants to sow division and discord. I agree with Peter Wagner when he says, "I do not believe we should see spiritual warfare as an end in itself… Jesus came to destroy the works of the devil (see 1 John 3:8), but this was only a means toward the end of seeking and saving that which was lost."[10] God's purpose is always to set the captives free, and we have been privileged to participate in this mission with Him.

The enemy of our soul wants to prevent us from being all that God has called us to be. He wants to keep us from completing those ...*good works which God prepared in advance for us to do* (Ephesians 2:10). But thank God ...*the one who is in you is greater than the one who is in the world* (1 John 4:4). And through Him, no matter what storms the enemy may stir up against us, we have the victory.

"And I will ask the Father, and he will give you another Counselor to be with you forever—the Spirit of truth. The world cannot accept him, because it neither sees him nor knows him. But you know him, for he lives with you and will be in you."

—John 14:16-17

CHAPTER FIVE

KEEPING THE WIND
IN YOUR SAILS

BILLY GRAHAM WROTE, "MAN HAS TWO GREAT spiritual needs. One is for forgiveness. The other is for goodness. Consciously or unconsciously, his inner being longs for both. There are times when man actually cries for them, even though in his restlessness, confusion, loneliness, fear, and pressures he may not know what he is crying for. God heard that first cry for help, that cry for forgiveness, and answered it at Calvary… But God also heard our second cry, that cry for goodness, and answered it at Pentecost. God does not want us to come to Christ by faith, and then lead a life of defeat, discouragement, and dissension. Rather he wants to '*fulfill every desire for **goodness** and the work of faith with power; in order that the name of Jesus Christ may be glorified in you*' (2 Thess. 1:11-12)."[1]

One of the greatest challenges we face today is understanding the work of the Holy Spirit. As I pointed out in Chapter 4, even believers can be unaware of the unseen spiritual battle raging around us (and sometimes in us!). We learned that we must not be ignorant of the enemy's schemes. Conversely, we must not be ignorant of God's Spirit who lives in us and overcomes the evil spirits. Scripture declares emphatically, *He who is in you is greater than he who is in the world* (1 John 4:4 NKJV).

Understanding who this Person is who lives in us is fundamental to not only weathering our storms, but in coming through them stronger, more mature, and more prepared to do God's will. As I said before, just surviving the storm—crawling up on the beach on your hands and knees, ready to lie down and die—is *not* God's plan for you! Just saying, "I made it through," is not enough.

Keeping the Wind in Your Sails

You need to be able to say, "I made it through this trial, and I am ready for the next wind of God. I'm not just getting to the other side; I'm going to be stronger than the storm I went through, stronger than I was before I went through it."

The years 2002 to 2004 were very challenging and difficult for me. I've already mentioned that my wife, Jennifer, was struggling with multiple incurable diseases. And at that time the church had battled the city council for nearly nine months to get a permit to add onto our existing facility. So in addition to being involved in a difficult building project at the church, I was fervently seeking healing for Jennifer and caring for our five children.

It was a stormy time, and the storms seemed to gain more force every day. But I was determined that I was going to come through them stronger and more committed than ever to keep fighting the good fight of faith. And on the other side of the storm, I discovered newfound strength, greater victory, and increased understanding. I experienced a fresh wind from heaven.

Don't quit your own fight of faith! Don't alter your course! Don't tell God, "I've been through all I can take in this life, and I'm done. I'm going to chill now. I'm going to retire." No. Instead, you must say, "God, breathe on me. God, give me the fresh wind of your Spirit in my sails."

The word for Spirit in the Scriptures, in both the Hebrew and Greek, is the same word often used for "wind."[2] In fact, Jesus himself likens the Holy Spirit to the wind in His conversation with Nicodemus: *"You should not be surprised at my saying, 'You must be born again.' The wind blows wherever it pleases. You hear its sound, but you cannot tell where it comes from or where it is going. So it is with everyone born of the Spirit"* (John 3:7-8).

Jesus' description here emphasizes several important characteristics of this "wind": like the wind of nature, it is powerful, yet invisible. It is mysterious because we don't know where it comes from or where it goes. It is sovereign in its action: *"it blows wherever it pleases."* And we are absolutely dependent on it for our very salvation.

Later in the book of John, on the eve of His crucifixion, Jesus told the disciples that it was actually a good
thing that He was "going away" because He was going to
send them the Holy Spirit. *"...It is for your good that I am
going away. Unless I go away, the Counselor will not come
to you; but if I go, I will send him to you"* (John 16:7).

In his book, *The Promise*, Tony Evans imagines the
fears of the disciples that night and Jesus' response:

Jesus knew that after His resurrection, the disciples would need supernatural power to pull off
what He wanted them to do. And He knew
where they were going to get that power: from
the enabling, internal presence of the Holy Spirit.
Now this is very important because whenever the
disciples needed help, Jesus was always there.

When they were lonely and needed a friend,
Jesus was a faithful friend. When they were
discouraged and needed encouragement, Jesus
was there to encourage them and give them joy.
When they were defeated and needed to be picked
up, Jesus was there to pick them up. When they
were afraid out on the sea and wondering how

they were going to make it, Jesus could walk on the water and calm their fear.

Whatever these men needed, Jesus was there to provide. So when they heard that Jesus was leaving, the question on the floor was, "Who is going to help us?" That is, "Jesus, if we are going to keep on, who is going to help us when we are down and encourage us when we are discouraged? Who is going to strengthen us when we are weak? Who is going to lead us when we are confused? You did all that for us…"

Jesus' task on that night was to convince His fearful, confused followers that the Helper He was sending was just like Him, only this Helper would be able to do even more for them.

So Jesus told them, "I am going to leave you now. But I am going to send you Someone who is always going to be there for you. No matter what your problem, no matter what your circumstance, no matter what your trial…no matter what you come up against, this Helper will be with you."[3]

Jesus knew what lay ahead, and He knew that His disciples would need this Someone to help them through it. This same Helper desires to help you today, tomorrow, or whenever you face the storms that Jesus said are inevitable. And we must have this Holy Spirit moving in our lives if we have any hope of keeping the wind in our sails.

There is much confusion today surrounding the third person of the Trinity. Some may not have received much teaching or preaching on the Holy Spirit. Perhaps others were told that the Holy Spirit—His person, His gifts, and His power—are not for today. But that isn't true—they are for today! Oh, how we need Him today!

THE HOLY SPIRIT IS A PERSON

Let's be clear about one thing: the Holy Spirit is a person, not a power. That is not to say that He is not powerful. On the contrary, as we shall see! But He is not an impersonal force we are trying to tap into like the Jedi Knights in *Star Wars*! Benny Hinn speaks to this point in *Welcome, Holy Spirit*: "The Holy Spirit is so much more than a force or a power. I can tell you from personal experience that when you stop learning *about* the Holy Spirit and begin to *know Him* as a person, your life will never be the same."[4]

Jesus himself never referred to the Holy Spirit as "it"; He always referred to the Spirit as "He." So let's not approach the Holy Spirit like some kind of electrical outlet we're trying to plug into—though you will find He is able to give you quite a power surge! No, He is the third person of the Trinity, with all the attributes of personhood and divinity. He is no less God than the Father and the Son. And He is a divine person with whom we are, amazingly, invited to have fellowship.

So how do we enter into this fellowship?

BAPTIZED WITH THE HOLY SPIRIT

In Acts 1, Jesus gives His closing instructions to His disciples: *"Do not leave Jerusalem, but wait for the gift my Father promised, which you have heard me speak about. For John baptized with water, but in a few days you will be baptized with the Holy Spirit"* (Acts 1:4). The word for *baptized* in the Greek is *baptizo*, which means to be immersed in, literally to be "dip-dyed." For generations theologians have debated whether there is only one, or if there are two experiences, with the Holy Spirit in the believer's life. Many hold that the only baptism of the Spirit occurs when we receive Christ, that is, when we are converted. But the passage from Acts 1 suggests there is a second experience.

In John 20:19, 21-22, Jesus appears to His disciples after His resurrection: *On the evening of that first day of the week, when the disciples were together, with the doors locked for fear of the Jews, Jesus came and stood among them and said, "Peace be with you!... As the Father has sent me, I am sending you." And with that he breathed on them and said, "Receive the Holy Spirit."* This passage indicates that when Jesus breathed on them, they received the Holy Spirit; that is, there was now in that person's life receptivity to the Holy Spirit. Since the Trinity cannot be broken or separated, when you accept Christ, you must also receive the Holy Spirit.

But the word *baptizo* is different from the Greek word "receive." *Baptizo* means to be dyed, like cloth. To be completely changed by immersion. Not only do you now have the Spirit resident in your life—as you do at conversion—but you now have Him in dominion *over* your life.

Again, later in Acts, Jesus told His disciples, *"It is not for you to know the times or dates the Father has set by his own authority. But you will receive power when the Holy Spirit comes on you; and you will be my witnesses in Jerusalem, and in all Judea and Samaria, and to the ends of the earth"* (Acts 1:7-8).

Jesus' purpose was to make His disciples aware that as long as they lived, the presence, power, and authority of God would be in the now, in the moment in which each of us lives. In other words, as I am living my life, perhaps going through a difficult time, I don't have to refer just to what God did in the lions' den. I don't have to refer just to what He did in the fiery furnace with Shadrach, Meshach, and Abednego. These are encouraging things to remember, for sure. But I can refer to who God is today—in the now...this moment. He is an active God in my life—the authority in my life. I don't have to talk only about what happened yesterday. I can talk about what is happening right now.

Jesus didn't want us to know just a historical God. This is not to say that we don't know God by what He has done in history. But God is still active in history by

His Holy Spirit. He is active in your personal history. Jesus wants us to know that God in our now. That's why Jesus told the disciples to wait on the Holy Spirit. "Don't just talk about Me raising Lazarus from the tomb. Don't just refer to Me opening blind eyes. Don't just talk about Me making the paralytic walk. I want you to talk about what I am doing today. I am a resident God, a present God. And I am an ever-present help in times of trouble."

WAIT ON THE HOLY SPIRIT

Jesus told His disciples to "wait on the Holy Spirit." He knew how much they would need the third person of the Trinity. The Person of Christ came to bring us forgiveness, but then He told the disciples, "Now I am going to leave the Holy Spirit with you. You have forgiveness, and you have eternal life. But now you need my authority and my power." We are no longer waiting on the Holy Spirit to come; we now wait on Him to direct us, to counsel us.

Let's not forget that this is the very power Paul refers to in Ephesians as *his incomparably great power for us who believe. That power is like the working of his mighty strength, which he exerted in Christ when he raised him from the dead and seated him at his right hand in the heavenly realms...* (Ephesians 1:19-20). That is the power you have living in you right now!

The Holy Spirit is here—today. But the Church often does not know how to relate to Him. Many believers lose strength and courage because they are not possessed by His power. But the Holy Spirit desires to empower you to go through whatever you are going through. So how do we move in His power?

As I said, we are no longer waiting for the dispensation of the Holy Spirit. He is here. The Bible says, *Do you not know that your body is a temple of the Holy Spirit, who is in you... ?* (1 Corinthians 6:19). Yet, in another sense, we must still "wait" for Him. We must wait on His authority and His direction in our lives.

Because we are human beings and live in an "instant" society, when we want something, we want it now. In our 24/7 society, we have become accustomed to getting most of the things we want instantly. However, this is a very dangerous expectation of God.

Consider again Jesus' instructions to His disciples. He wasn't just teaching them a lesson about waiting; He also taught some valuable lessons about the purposes of waiting, which we need to learn as well.

FIND PURPOSE IN WAITING

It is very important and beneficial to find the purpose in waiting, because typically, what we have to wait for, we value more. But often we are in a hurry and get ahead of God. We begin to do things God does not want us to do.

Waiting is certainly counter-cultural. Not only because we live in a society that demands instant gratification, but also because the world is driven by pressure rather than purpose. "I've got to purchase this now. They told me it's a one-time offer, and the sale ends on Monday." If you're led by the Spirit, the offer can end on Monday, but it doesn't end then with the Holy Spirit! God will provide what you need. Don't give in to the world's pressures. If you are sure of your purpose, you will be able to wait.

WAIT FOR THE ANOINTING

Jesus also wants us to understand the connection between the Holy Spirit and the anointing. Luke 4 shows us the working of the Holy Spirit in Jesus' own life, at the beginning of His ministry. He had just been baptized by John in the Jordan River, and *the Holy Spirit descended on him in bodily form...* (Luke 3:22). Luke 4:1-2 tells us that Jesus returned from His baptism *full of the Holy Spirit.* He was then *led by the Spirit,* as we discussed in Chapter 2, into the desert to be tempted by Satan. Later He returned from those forty days in the wilderness *in the power of the Spirit* (v. 14).

Jesus then went into the synagogue in His hometown and read from this passage found also in Isaiah 61:

> *"The Spirit of the Lord is on me, because he has **anointed** me to preach good news to the poor. He has sent me to proclaim freedom for the prisoners and recovery of sight for the blind, to release the oppressed, to proclaim the year of the Lord's favor." Then he rolled up the scroll, gave it back to the attendant and sat down. The eyes of everyone in the synagogue were fastened on him, and he began by saying to them,*

*"Today this scripture is fulfilled in your hearing." All
spoke well of him and were amazed at the gracious
words that came from his lips...*
—Luke 4:18-19, 21, emphasis added

In his book entitled *The Anointing*, R. T. Kendall
simply defines the anointing like this: "The anointing is
the power of the Holy Spirit. At the end of the day there
is no better definition."[5]

In the above scripture passage, we see that Jesus was
anointed by the Spirit at His baptism, during His temptation, and in the synagogue, where He told His listeners,
"the Spirit of the Lord...has anointed me." His listeners'
response was one of awe at His "gracious words."

We need the anointing no less in our own lives. And
Jesus has promised us that anointing. He wants us to
understand that there is a big difference between speech
and anointed speech...evangelism and anointed evangelism...preaching and anointed preaching. We have
all probably experienced times when we felt our words
came together easily, or we felt a special "touch of God."
We say to ourselves, "I felt different. I felt empowered.
I felt bold when I spoke." That is the anointing. The

anointing, Kendall points out, makes our gifts "function with ease."[6]

When you wait on the Lord, He will anoint you and give you boldness to speak. Don't misunderstand me; we do not control the Holy Spirit. As Jesus told Nicodemus in John 3, "The Spirit blows where it pleases." But we must always seek His fresh anointing. If Jesus needed that anointing, how much more should we seek it? We must be inseparable from the Holy Spirit.

WAITING HONORS GOD

Jesus wants us to wait on the Holy Spirit in order to honor God. Jesus told the disciples, "Wait because My Father is going to give you the gift." They waited because they wanted to honor the mandate of God. They wanted to honor what Jesus had said.

When I pray about something that I want to do, and I don't sense the release of the Spirit to do it, oftentimes I just need to remember that I must wait on the Lord. This honors the Word of God.

The Bible tells us that our waiting on God will strengthen, not weaken, us. Many of us are familiar with this beautiful passage from Isaiah:

*He gives power to the weak, and to those who have no might He increases strength. Even the youths shall faint and be weary, and the young men shall utterly fall, but those who **wait on the** LORD *shall renew their strength; they shall mount up with wings like eagles, they shall run and not be weary, they shall walk and not faint.*

—Isaiah 40:29-31 NKJV, emphasis added

This passage is for the storm-tossed, the trial-weary. It says that even the young and strong will collapse under the pressures of this life; our strength is not in our youth, or in ourselves. Our strength comes from waiting on God. This waiting honors Him with our faith, and He answers us by empowering us with the Holy Spirit so we can face our storms.

WANTING THE HOLY SPIRIT

To keep the wind in our sails, there must also be in us a wanting, a desire. We must have something we are anticipating, something we are believing for. That desire keeps us hungry for the Spirit, who keeps our walk with God fresh.

If I just went to church because the Bible told me to go, eventually I would burn out. But because the Holy Spirit operates in my life, I go to church with anticipation and excitement.

I was saved in 1977, and baptized in the Spirit in 1978. For one year, I lived by the rules. That's how I thought I should live to please God. I did not understand the Holy Spirit, and sometimes when we don't understand Him, we become legalistic. But the Holy Spirit will take that legalism out of us! When the Holy Spirit rules our lives, our walk is not all about performing according to the rules. When we are led by the Spirit, we have His power to lead lives that are pleasing to God—and to us.

Jesus wants us to experience a continual freshness in our relationship with God. The disciples wanted Jesus to remain with them. In fact, Peter even said, "I won't let You go. I don't want You to die"; to which Jesus made this remarkable reply: *"Get behind me, Satan!"* (Matthew 16:23). Jesus knew the work He had come to accomplish at Calvary and at Pentecost. In other words, Jesus was saying, "I must die and go to my Father. Then I will send you Another with authority and power. And then, instead of just working through Me, He will work through you—and you will do greater things than I have done."

I graduated from Oral Roberts University in Tulsa, Oklahoma. The university is situated on what was once a desolate tract of farmland. But one day the Holy Spirit spoke to Oral Roberts about His purpose for that land: "I want you to build a university on God's authority and the Holy Spirit to raise up your students to hear My voice, to go where My Light is dim, where My voice is heard small, and My healing power is not known, even to the uttermost bounds of the earth. Their work will exceed yours, and in this I am well pleased." Oral Roberts obeyed the Holy Spirit's commission, and thousands of young men and women have been raised up and sent out, taking God's Word all over the world.

Our relationship with the Holy Spirit is not only exciting, but it also grants us many privileges. The Holy Spirit has given us gifts (see 1 Corinthians 12). Through the Holy Spirit, we have the mind of Christ.

Tony Evans writes, "The Holy Spirit is absolutely central to the Christian life. And yet…a great deal of confusion has been connected to the work of the Holy Spirit. This has led to a lot of misappropriation, as well as a lot of gross *under* appropriation of His power and gifts."[7]

When we know who this Spirit is who lives in us, we declare the words of God with boldness. As Peter says, *If anyone speaks, he should do it as one speaking the very words of God* (1 Peter 4:11). We should be an oracle of God!

Helen Keller once said, "One can never consent to creep when one feels an impulse to soar."[8] God's Word says that if we wait on Him, we will soar like eagles. And our desire should be like Michelangelo's, who prayed this prayer, "Lord, grant that I may always desire more than I can accomplish."[9] In other words, Lord propel me with a fresh desire to always live beyond the moment, so that by Your power, I can also take others beyond.

THE POWER OF GOD

The disciples knew something about the power of God. They saw it in the life and ministry of Jesus. They experienced some of it. And Jesus promised them they would receive power when He sent the Holy Spirit. But we need to be clear about the purpose of that power. Jesus had to remind the disciples not to get too caught up in the manifestations of power:

> *The seventy-two returned with joy and said, "Lord, even the demons submit to us in your name." He replied, "I saw Satan fall like lightning from heaven. I have given you authority to trample on snakes and scorpions and to overcome all the power of the enemy; nothing will harm you. However, do not rejoice that the spirits submit to you, but rejoice that your names are written in heaven."*
>
> —Luke 10:17-20

In the same way, believers today often think the power of the Holy Spirit is all about casting out demons or being slain in the Spirit. Many believers seem to think that the power of the Holy Spirit is exclusively about the exhibition of that power. But the Holy Spirit's power is for so much more: His power enables you and me to lead holy lives, lives that are led by Him and bear the fruit of His presence.

The Holy Spirit empowers me to love you when you don't love me. The Holy Spirit empowers me to forgive you when you have deeply wronged me. The Holy Spirit empowers me to bless you when you curse me. The Holy Spirit empowers us to lead lives without bitterness, anger, malice, or unforgiveness.

Bill Bright expresses this truth succinctly: "The Holy Spirit is not given to us that we might have a great emotional experience, but that we might live super-naturally—holy lives—and be fruitful witnesses for Christ."[10]

Answering a question about the Holy Spirit, Campus Crusade for Christ, International's EveryStudent.com provided this response: "The Holy Spirit was given to live inside those who believe in Jesus, in order to produce God's character in the life of a believer. In a way that we cannot do on our own, the Holy Spirit will build into our lives love, joy, peace, patience, kindness, goodness, faithfulness, gentleness, and self-control (Gal. 5:22-23). Rather than trying to be loving, patient, and kind, God asks us to rely on Him to produce these qualities in our lives. Thus Christians are told to walk in the Spirit (Gal. 5:25) and be filled with the Spirit (Eph. 5:18)".[11]

THE PRESENCE OF GOD

The Spirit of God also brings the presence of God. Jesus knew that His disciples needed this presence. After all, these were the same disciples who were concerned about *"Who is the greatest in the kingdom of heaven?"* (Matthew 18:1). Two chapters later, the mother of James and John asks Jesus if her two boys can sit on His right and His left in His kingdom (see Matthew 20:21). The disciples were concerned about position rather than presence.

The Holy Spirit is not just God's power but also His very presence in our lives. Jesus told the disciples, "You're going to receive power, and My presence is going to be with you." They carried the presence of God in them, and became God's hands extended. Jesus said, *"... [You] will lay hands on the sick, and they will recover"* (Mark 16:18 NKJV). Even Peter's shadow falling on a man had the power to heal him.

Romans 8:9 says we are to be led or controlled by the Holy Spirit. If this is true, then our lives will show forth the fruit of that Spirit, and other people will see God's presence in us.

Those very attributes will be the strength we need to get to the other side of our storms without bitterness, anger, or self-pity. We can get to the other side of the crisis without saying, "I quit," when we have the power and the presence of the Holy Spirit. That's what keeps the wind in our sails.

WILLINGNESS

In 1981, after being out of high school for six years, I had a great desire to attend Oral Roberts University. I knew that my ACT scores were not good enough to get me in...without a miracle. And I certainly didn't have the money to pay tuition for four years. But having felt the hand of God on my life to preach, I knew that I needed training, so I had to be willing to trust God for acceptance to the university and for the finances to pay for it.

Even after God performed the miracle, and I was accepted, it was a real exercise in faith to depend on Him to provide the needed funds. Human nature is more comfortable knowing that there is a financial plan in place to cover the costs. But that was not the case in my situation, so I enrolled in a summer course, even though I didn't have the money to pay for it. I started attending classes, trusting that God would make a way.

One day, the professor read off the names of the students who hadn't yet paid for the course, but my name wasn't on the list. At the end of class, I asked the professor to check the list again, assuring him that I had not paid for the course. It was the only right thing to do—after all it was a Bible course. He told me I would have to take it up with the business office because as far as he was concerned, I was paid. When I checked with the business office, they told me that someone had paid in full for me to take the course. To this day I don't know who that person was.

My willingness to trust God, even though it would have been more comfortable to know ahead of time that the funds were there, placed me in the position of receiving from Him. God had assured me that I would graduate debt free, and on the day of our graduation ceremony, I received enough cash gifts to cover the remaining debt I owed for my college education. I'm telling you—your willingness to trust God can propel you beyond your storms—financial or otherwise!

When you have waited and wanted, then you will be willing. You will not be attached any longer to your own agenda. You will no longer rule your life when you have waited on the Spirit of God. When the apostle Peter— the very same man who declared that Jesus must not be crucified and then denied Him three times—received the Holy Spirit, his will changed. He released his life to the Lord, was used mightily of Him, and even followed the Lord in crucifixion. When the Holy Spirit comes upon us, we identify with God's desires and responsibilities, and we begin to conform to the very image of Jesus and what He was willing to do for us. The Holy Spirit helps us detach from our wills and attach ourselves to His will.

If we aren't attached to God's will, usually we become attached to what we're comfortable with. I'm comfortable with a certain way of worship. I'm comfortable with a certain kind of preaching. I'm comfortable with where I live. I'm comfortable with my job. But we are not called to be comfortable in that sense. The Holy

Spirit is the Comforter; He is not "comfortable." He is taking us from glory to glory and causing us to grow.

Not long ago, during one of our Oklahoma storms—not a tornado but one with straight winds of 85 miles per hour—I looked out the window to see our new trampoline, one with wheels on it, taking off across our yard into the neighboring wheat field. My daughter, Victoria, the one—you may remember—who hates storms, was watching with me, but rather than being afraid, she had to laugh at the sight. As the person who was going to have to retrieve this trampoline, however, I began thinking, *Once this storm is over, I'll bolt that trampoline to the ground, so this never happens again.* The Holy Spirit spoke to me and said, "If you do that, it will break. As it is now, it's just a little misplaced." This is a good lesson for us in our spiritual lives as well.

We can get so tied to our own agendas or to our own comfort, that when the wind of the Spirit blows, rather than moving with it, we break. My trampoline was just fine, by the way.

LEADING OF THE HOLY SPIRIT

The only way we can do anything good, anything that will last, is by the authority and leading of the Holy Spirit. He is the only way. Jesus knew that His disciples would get worn down from the criticism, opposition, and adversity—all the storms that come to shake us. He said, "You need the wind of the Holy Spirit. You need the Holy Spirit to keep your life free and fluid and responsive to Me."

Keep His freshening wind in your sails. Allow Him to have His rule and dominion over your life. That does not mean that the storms will pass you by, but it does mean that the Holy Spirit will be with you.

Therefore, do not throw away your confidence,
which has a great reward. For you have need of
endurance, so that when you have done the will
of God, you may receive what was promised.

—Hebrews 10:35-36 NASU

CHAPTER SIX

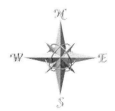

STORM DEBRIEFING

L IKE DEATH AND TAXES, THE STORMS OF LIFE are a certainty. Jesus predicted that *"...here on earth you will have many trials and sorrows..."* (John 16:33 NLT). But as we have seen, He has left us with the most trustworthy guide and guidebook to see us safely through each one. We have examined scriptural principles for mastering our storms, for staying on course in the midst of storms, and for getting to the other side of the storms, strengthened, seasoned, and with renewed commitment to God's ongoing purposes for our lives.

In this final chapter, I will show you how to process your storm in a way that enables you to move on in your life and keep running the ...*race marked out for us* (Hebrews 12:1). Sometimes when the storm has subsided, we find that we have lost our strength, our energy, and even our will to go on. We say things like, "I did everything I could to keep our marriage together." "I did everything I could to keep him, or her, alive." "I did everything I could to hang on to my job." "I did everything I could to raise my kids right." "I did everything I could to avoid depression." "I did everything I could, and I have nothing left."

Don't embrace this wrong thinking—challenge it! There is a reservoir of God in your life if you are a Christian. As we saw in the last chapter, you have the same Spirit inside you that raised Jesus from the dead! There is more in you than you have begun to imagine. *If God is for us, who can be against us?* (Romans 8:31).

Sometimes we need a good housecleaning after a storm. We need to air out the house. We need to unbolt some of those closets in our souls that have signs saying, "Do Not Enter!" When we clear out what's in those closets—fear, fatigue, and flaws—we find that we suddenly have room for more of God. If we get rid of the anger, we have more room for joy. If we get rid of the turmoil, there's more room for peace. Once we start sorting through, processing all the "stuff," there will be a new sense of spaciousness, more freedom and openness, and even laughter again.

Even for those of us who have lost someone very dear, our lives are not over. Our destiny is not derailed. When I was at Evelyn Roberts' funeral in May 2005, Oral Roberts stood to speak. We all held our breath because he was not scheduled to do so. "I loved my darling wife Evelyn"—as he always called her—"but I am not done," he said. Goosebumps went from the top of my head to the soles of my feet. As long as you have breath and life, you are not finished. God has plans—good plans—for your life.

Perhaps someone along the way has told you that you are finished—that you're going to be disenfranchised, disinherited, divorced, or discounted. There is debris all along the pathway of your yesterdays, but there is hope on the pathway of your tomorrows.

Listen to what David Wilkerson said from the pulpit of the Times Square Church in New York:

Paul then sums it up with this word: *This one thing I do, forgetting those things which are behind, and reaching forth unto those things which are before* (Philippians 3:13 KJV). In short, he thought it was impossible to place his future into the Lord's hands without first laying down his past. There could be no regrets, no reliving past sins and failures, no wondering what could have been.

Like Paul, I now look forward to my tomorrows, because I know my Father cares...that he keeps his Word...that he works all things together for my good...that he is with me and will never forsake me...that his eye is on me, and his thoughts toward me are good...that His promises cannot fail. I urge you: trust the Lord with all your tomorrows...[1]

I want you to be in this very position at the end of your storm—looking ahead with hope and trusting God with all your tomorrows. To that end, I am listing six steps for debriefing after your storm. I believe these steps will help you come through your storm in ways the world (and maybe even you) least expects—whole, healthy, strong, and with more love for the Lord Jesus Christ.

Let's begin by looking at a story from the book of Judges. This is the story of Jephthah, an unlikely biblical hero—but then so many of them are unlikely in the world's terms, aren't they?

> *Jephthah the Gileadite was a mighty warrior. His father was Gilead; his mother was a prostitute. Gilead's wife also bore him sons, and when they were grown up, they drove Jephthah away. "You are not going to get any inheritance in our family," they said, "because you are the son of another woman." So Jephthah fled from his brothers and settled in the land of Tob, where a group of adventurers gathered around him and followed him.*
>
> *Some time later, when the Ammonites made war on Israel, the elders of Gilead went to get Jephthah from the land of Tob. "Come," they said, "be our commander so we can fight the Ammonites."*

Jephthah said to them, "Didn't you hate me and drive me from my father's house? Why do you come to me now, when you're in trouble?"

The elders of Gilead said to him, "Nevertheless, we are turning to you now; come with us to fight the Ammonites, and you will be our head over all who live in Gilead."

Jephthah answered, "Suppose you take me back to fight the Ammonites and the Lord gives them to me—will I really be your head?"

The elders of Gilead replied, "The LORD is our witness; we will certainly do as you say." So Jephthah went with the elders of Gilead, and the people made him head and commander over them. And he repeated all his words before the LORD in Mizpah.

—Judges 11:1-11

Jephthah the Gileadite was a mighty warrior. His father was Gilead; his mother was a prostitute. Not a very encouraging beginning, is it? Can you imagine standing up in school and telling the class that your mom did that for a living? Worse, Gilead's dad had other sons, with his legal wife, who obviously hated their illegitimate half-brother because, *when they were grown up, they drove Jephthah away.*

In three short verses the Bible summarized the storm of Jephthah's life. His mother was a prostitute. His half-brothers hated him and drove him off, so he couldn't receive any of his father's inheritance. "I have no place in my family, no protection from my father, no inheritance, and my future has been decreed by my malevolent half-brothers."

His brothers told him, *"You are not going to get any inheritance…because you are the son of another woman."* And not just any woman—a prostitute. That had to hurt. That had to get inside his thinking about himself. That had to crawl inside his spirit. He might have been a "great warrior"—even a John Wayne—but that would still hurt deeply.

Do you know what the devil wants to sell you today? Or sell you as? He wants you to think you are damaged goods. "We couldn't get anything for you on the shelf; we're putting you on clearance." That is another lie straight from hell.

God didn't create damaged goods. Yes, life sometimes damages us by inflicting wounds on us. But God is waiting to raise you up, to put the passion back in your soul. This story of Jephthah is an encouragement for all of us who have ever counted ourselves out.

So Jephthah fled from his brothers and settled in the land of Tob, where a group of adventurers gathered around him and followed him. Jephthath may have had to flee his brothers, but look at what happened. He may have been the son of a prostitute, and he may have been disinherited, but the Scripture says that a band of *adventurers gathered around him and followed him.* The word for "adventurers" here is the same word used to describe the men who followed David when he was fleeing from Saul. They were men, like Jephthah, who had fallen on hard times, but they saw something in Jephthah that drew them.

Whenever God's hand is on your life, you cannot keep people away from you. It doesn't matter what others may say about you—"you son of a prostitute!" When God is in you and leading your life, there will be people who want to be around you. When God's hand is on your life, it doesn't matter where you land. Someone will be waiting for God's man or woman—they will be there for them.

But let's look at what happened next. The Ammonites attacked Israel, and suddenly the brothers come to Jephthah for help. This is where Jephthah begins his debriefing. He had been thrown out of his house, driven away, disinherited, and yet at the first sign of trouble, "the elders of Gilead" appealed to him for help. Why? Because they knew that war was imminent and that there was a mighty anointing on Jephthah's life.

You should not think it strange that storms assail you. If you are a Christian, there is a call on your life. You were created in the image and likeness of God, and you are meant to bear His love and character in a lost and dying world. It's hardly surprising, then, that the devil wants you out of the picture. But there is a destiny in you that overshadows the devil's destructive plan.

Jephthah started the debriefing by asking some questions. "Didn't you hate me and drive me from my father's house? Why do you come to me now, when you're in trouble?" Jephthah then asks them, "If I come with you, and if the Lord gives me victory, will you really make me ruler over all the people?"

*The elders of Gilead replied, "The LORD is our witness; we will certainly do as you say." So Jephthah went with the elders of Gilead, and the people made him head and commander over them. **And he repeated all his words before the LORD in Mizpah.***

Judges 11:10–11, emphasis added

Don't miss that last line. Jephthah was in the presence of the Lord. After all he had endured, all the storms he had come through, he had not become bitter and alienated. Things must have looked pretty hopeless, but Jephthah didn't give up.

No matter what you feel like, no matter how grim or hopeless things may seem, God has promised that He will never leave you or forsake you. Even when we don't feel His presence, we still must stand on the truth of God's Word. As I said before, we do not, as Christians, live our lives based on our feelings. We live them based on the truth of God. So no matter who attacks us, no matter who assaults us, no matter who betrays us, God still wants us and still has a call on each of us.

Let's skip ahead in our story. *Then Jephthah sent messengers to the Ammonite king with the question: "What do you have against us that you have attacked our country?"* (v. 12). *The king of Ammon, however, paid no attention to the message Jephthah sent him. Then the Spirit of the Lord came upon Jephthah. He crossed Gilead and Mannaseh…and from there he advanced against the Ammonites* (vv. 28-29).

It doesn't matter what other people think of you or what they have predicted for your life, as long as you don't change what you think about what God thinks about you. That's truth. "People have told me I'll never amount to anything. Nothing good is ever going to happen. And based on all the storms in my life, they must be right." No! Do not ever measure yourself by anyone else's measure. Look to God and His measurement for your life. And do not measure your future by your storms. Measure your future only by the unshakeable Word of God.

SIX PRINCIPLES FOR STORM DEBRIEFING

Let's look at some steps now to help you process your storms and come through them ready for the next wind of God.

1. Do a spiritual appraisal

The first step in storm cleanup is to do a spiritual appraisal. We need to take a look at what the storm has turned up in our lives. In other words, has this adversity made me bitter or better? There was in a time in my own life when adversity produced only bitterness. I learned how to share my story of what a victim I was. Storms washed up all kinds of ugly things on the beach of my soul.

We need to keep ourselves on a short leash by doing daily appraisals. We need to get up every morning and say, "God, I want to look in the mirror of Your Spirit. I want You to show me who I am and what I am thinking." This is a good habit to cultivate, because when the storms of life come, this kind of appraisal will keep you from being filled with bitterness, resentment, and self-pity.

We need to look deep inside ourselves, with the help of the Holy Spirit, as David did in Psalm 51. Sometimes, however, we are blind to our wrong attitudes, and then we need a Nathan to come alongside us (see 2 Samuel 12). If you can't hear from the Holy Ghost, then ask the Lord to send you a Nathan, someone who will reveal the needed truth.

2. Be honest with yourself

The second step is to be honest about what the Spirit reveals to you. Sometimes that is easier said than done. How do we get honest with ourselves? I usually like to go through the names of people I know. If there's a name that bothers me, I keep bringing that name up because, of course, it represents a person. If I asked you right now the name of your ex-husband or ex-wife, would that name evoke some kind of hurt in your life? Maybe it's the name of your ex-boss, or a sibling, parent, neighbor, or friend that distresses you. God does not want you to feel pain any longer when you think of that name.

So when I do a spiritual appraisal, especially after a difficult time in my life, I begin to pray for the names and the people they represent. I say, "God, I bless them.

They ill-used me or persecuted me, but Your Word says to bless those who persecute me. So, God, I bless them, and I ask You to bless them." Then the devil gets confused and has to go to counseling! "Wait a minute. I sent that person to destroy that Christian's life and faith. And now they're blessing them?"

Do an appraisal and clear out that spiritual closet. Get rid of the things that don't fit anymore. Hatred doesn't fit anymore. It doesn't go on right. Anger doesn't fit anymore. Bitterness doesn't fit me anymore either.

Do an honest spiritual appraisal, and don't make excuses. Often, when we honestly admit something we did that we shouldn't have, we immediately try to get ourselves off the hook. "I shouldn't have said that, but they shouldn't have said what they said either! I shouldn't have done that—but they shouldn't have done that either." Yes, but that is just excusing yourself. Our model must be our Lord—beaten, scourged, crucified, yet as He hung there on the cross, He said, "Father, forgive them." Jesus said, "I am going to take on the sins of the world. What they are doing to Me, I am not going to do to them." In His moment of appraisal in the Garden,

Jesus asked the Father, "If it be Your will, let this cup pass from Me. But if it is not, then so be it."

So in our own lives, we must ask God to take the things from us that Jesus has already taken. We must ask God to do the things that Jesus has already done. We need to say to ourselves, "I am not going to carry that hurt or those wounds. Jesus is going to carry that."

Jephthah could have told those men, his brothers, that he had no intention of helping them. Instead, he did an honest appraisal. "Aren't you the guys who threw me out? Called my mother a prostitute?" He could have said then, "Okay, now pay the price. I have no intention of bailing you out." That would be the sign of a wounded soul. Instead, because of the call on his life, (remember the Bible calls him a "great warrior"), Jephthah chose to forgive them and walk in his anointing. That's the sign of an honest spiritual appraisal.

3. Establish a spiritual standard by which to measure your life

As we have seen, the question certainly is not whether we will encounter storms. The question is who will we be when we reach the other side of storms? If we live our lives by the standards of the Word of God, no storm can destroy us. There is no storm big enough to take you down if you are submitted to biblical standards. When it is time to repent, then repent. When it's time to forgive, forgive. When it's time to bless, bless. When it's time to let go, let go. When it's time to give your coat, give your coat. When it's time to go the second mile, go the second mile. Determine to live your life by the standards of Jesus.

David Culver tells of watching a TV news report on the damage inflicted by Hurricane Andrew:

In one scene, amid the devastation and debris stood one house on its foundation. The owner was cleaning up the yard when a reporter approached him.

"Sir, why is your house the only one still standing?" asked the reporter. "How did you manage to escape the severe damage of the hurricane?"

"I built this house myself," the man replied. "I also built it according to the Florida state building code. When the code called for 2x6 roof trusses, I used 2x6 trusses. I was told that a house built according to code could withstand a hurricane. I did, and it did. I suppose no one else around here followed the code."[2]

Total damage caused by Hurricane Andrew exceeded $20 billion. During cleanup, building inspectors surveying the damaged homes found that many were not built to code. Construction had been done with trusses that were missing hurricane straps, and staples had been used instead of nails for securing shingles. Houses built with shoddy construction crumbled when faced with the force of the storm.

There is a building code for our lives as well. We have a Bible code that gives us foundational principles upon which to construct our lives.

If you want to stay debris-free, listen to the Word of God. The Bible tells us not to forsake the assembling of ourselves together (see Hebrews 10:25). That's a Bible code. You can't get around it by saying, "I'm hurt. I'm wounded. I can't go to church." You need to be in a house of worship.

In Luke 6:38, Jesus says, *"Give, and it will be given to you. A good measure, pressed down, shaken together and running over, will be poured into your lap."* The Bible also says, *"Bring the whole tithe into the storehouse..."* (Malachi 3:10). These are part of the Bible code, and if I build my life using these 2x6 trusses, I can withstand the day of trouble.

4. Seek godly counsel and wisdom

We have already discussed the importance of godly wisdom in Chapter 1. There I pointed out the importance of allowing godly people to speak into our lives in the midst of our storms. Godly counsel is just as significant in debriefing after the storms are over. We need to make sure that none of the debris from the storm—bitterness, unforgiveness, doubt, anger, or wrong thinking—has lodged in our souls.

I have several friends whom I turn to for counsel on a regular basis, but especially when I am going through a difficult time. I ask them to help me gain perspective, because I am not worried about being right—I desire to be righteous. I don't want anything negative or hurtful to be left in my life to be passed on to someone else. So it is often wise to turn to other believers you trust to help gain a more objective perspective about how the storm has affected you.

5. Access spiritual strength

We access spiritual strength by being in the presence of God. Often we settle for natural acceptance—the approval or acceptance of our friends or family. That makes us think we don't need God's presence. But it wasn't enough for Jephthah to have the approval of his band of followers. Acceptance will never bring us the strength we need to face our next storm. At the end of the day, it's God's acceptance we need. And we already have His vote. So stay in His presence, and get around others who stay in His presence too.

Jephthah had done the right spiritual appraisal. I am convinced that he did because he asked the right questions. "Why do you want me back? Aren't you the ones who hated me and drove me away?" He asked the questions that would have hurt most people to ask. We don't ask, "Why did you hate me?" because we don't want to hear the reason or to hear that perhaps they still do! But Jephthah said, "I don't care. I just want to know. You want me back because you are going through trouble?

Okay, I'll come. You can deal with your own issues. I don't have any. I just want to help the people of God. I know I am a great warrior and called to battle." He had the spiritual strength to do what was needed and to fulfill his destiny.

6. Have a right spiritual attitude

Philippians 2:5-8 says, *Your attitude should be the same as that of Christ Jesus: Who being in very nature God, did not consider equality with God something to be grasped, but made himself nothing, taking the very nature of a servant...he humbled himself and became obedient to death—even death on a cross!*

Finally, you must be possessed of a right attitude. Jesus modeled that attitude for us. Though He was God, He submitted himself wholly to His Father's will, even though it meant a torturous, shameful death on the cross. We are called to be like Jesus. We have been *predestined,* Scripture tells us, *...to be conformed to the likeness of his Son...* (Romans 8:29).

So when we come through the storm and are standing on the opposite shore, we must do an attitude check. Is our attitude towards God "the same as that of Christ

Jesus?" Are we humble, willing, and obedient? Are we submitted to Him in whatever is ahead?

You and I have the Holy Spirit. Jesus said that He would leave Him for us. Acts 2:17-18 tells us: *"In the last days, God says, I will pour out my Spirit on all people...Even on my servants, both men and women, I will pour out my Spirit in those days..."*

The question we must ask ourselves is, "Does the Holy Spirit have us...all of us?"

Billy Graham puts it like this: "When we are filled with the Spirit, it is not a question of there being more of Him, as though His work in us is quantitative. It is not how much of the Spirit we have, but how much the Spirit has of us."[3]

Friends, the storms of life will come. The rains will fall, the streams will rise, and the winds will blow. But will your house be built upon the rock or upon the sand? Jesus says if we hear His words and *put them into practice,* we will be like the wise man whose house withstood the storm because its foundation was built on the rock.

No matter where you are at this moment—in the midst of the most difficult time of your life, or emerging from a trial weary and battered—God has not left your side. He will never withdraw His love, His help, or His good plans for your future. He is still the master of the storm—He still *"commands even the winds and the water, and they obey Him!"* (Luke 8:25 NKJV). So come unto Him in trust and faith. Let Him lead you through the storm—through what only seems like darkness—to the other side, confident that He who began a good work in you will bring it to a glorious conclusion.

Dear brothers and sisters, whenever trouble comes your way, let it be an opportunity for joy. For when your faith is tested, your endurance has a chance to grow. So let it grow, for when your endurance is fully developed, you will be strong in character and ready for anything.

—James 1:2-3 NLT

NOTES

Chapter One

1. Rick Warren, "*Preparing for Eternity: On Purpose—A Conversation with Rick Warren,*" Interview by Jim Dailey, *Decision* magazine (November 2004), 28.

2. Elisabeth Elliot, *Secure in God's Everlasting Arms* (Ann Arbor: Servant Publications, 2002), 51.

3. Ibid., 71.

4. Clift Richards, *God's Special Promises to Me* (Tulsa: Victory House, 1996), 21-22.

5. Rick Warren, *The Purpose Driven Life* (Grand Rapids: Zondervan, 2002), 110-111.

Chapter Two

1. Leo Harris, *Five Keys to Authority* (Fullerton: Crusader Publications, n.d.), 22-23.

2. Trent C. Butler, ed. "Entry for 'HEART'", *Holman Bible Dictionary*, http://www.studylight.org/dic/hbd/view.cgi?number=T654>.1991.

3. Trent C. Butler, ed., "Entry for 'HOPE'", *Holman Bible Dictionary*, http://www.studylight.org/dic/hbd/view.cgi?number=T2841>.1991.

Chapter Three

1. Rick Warren, *The Purpose Driven Life* (Grand Rapids: Zondervan, 2002), 32.

2. Os Guinness, *The Call* (Nashville: Word Publishing, 1998), 170.

3. Rick Warren, *The Purpose Driven Life*, 28.

4. Gerald Coates, *The Vision* (Eastbourne: Kingsway Publications, 1995), 21.

5. Ibid., 25.

6. Os Guinness, *The Call*, 243.

7. Ibid., 31.

8. Ibid., 47.

9. Dorothy Sayers, "Why Work?", *Creed or Chaos* (New York: Harcourt, Brace, 1949), 53.

10. Ibid., 57.

Chapter Four

1. Michael Youssef, *Know Your Real Enemy* (Nashville: Thomas Nelson Publishers, 1997), 7.

2. Ibid., 11.

3. Neil T. Anderson and Timothy M. Warner, *The Beginner's Guide to Spiritual Warfare* (Ventura: Regal Books, 2000), 77.

4. Ibid., 81.

5. Ibid., 80.

6. John Bevere, *The Bait of Satan* (Lake Mary: Charisma House, 2004), 6.

7. Ibid., 2.

8. C. Peter Wagner, *Warfare Prayer: How to Seek God's Power and Protection in the Battle to Build His Kingdom* (Ventura: Regal, 1992), 88.

9. Ibid., 76-77.

10. Ibid., 20.

Chapter Five

1. Billy Graham, *The Holy Spirit* (Dallas: Word Publishing, 1988), 11.

2. Ibid., 24.

3. Tony Evans, *The Promise* (Chicago: Moody Press, 1996), 24-25.

4. Benny Hinn, *Welcome, Holy Spirit* (Nashville: Thomas Nelson Publishers, 1997), 28.

5. R. T. Kendall, *The Anointing* (Nashville: Thomas Nelson Publishers, 1999), 3.

6. Ibid., 4.

7. Tony Evans, *The Promise* (Chicago: Moody Press, 1996), 16.

8. Helen Keller, *The Book of Positive Quotations*, Compiled by John Cook, (New York: Random House, Gramercy Books, 1999), 334.

9. Michelangelo, *Wise Words and Quotes*, Vern McLellan, (Wheaton: Tyndale House Publishers, 1998), 2.

10. Bill Bright, *The Holy Spirit* (San Bernardino: New Life Publications, 1980), 84.
11. "Who is the Holy Spirit?" EveryStudent.com http://www. everystudent.com/forum/hspirit.html.

Chapter Six
1. David Wilkerson, "Trusting God with All Your Tomorrows," Times Square Pulpit Series, May 22, 2006.
2. David Culver, "Obedience," *Leadership* 14, no. 1 (Winter 1993), 49.
3. Billy Graham, *The Holy Spirit*, 100.

ABOUT THE AUTHOR

MARK CROW, ALONG WITH HIS WIFE, Jennifer, pastor Victory Church, in Oklahoma City, which they founded in 1994. Mark's ministry philosophy was not to build a church, but to build people to live life victoriously in Jesus. With over 8,000 members, 12,000 decisions for Christ, and planting churches in other cities across America, Mark's motto, "You were born for victory," is reflected not on a church wall, but on the hearts and in the lives of men and women.

For information on the weekly TV show, "The Art of Living," or information about Mark Crow and Victory Church, visit the church's Web site at:

www.victorychurch.tv

Victory Church is located at 4300 North MacArthur, Oklahoma City, OK 73122.

VICTORY
CHURCH.TV

The Art of Living weekly TV show is broadcast on the
Daystar Network in over 130 countries. Visit our Web site
at www.victorychurch.tv for local times and listings.

The following are available wherever fine books are sold.

Secrets of the Second Mile
How to Overcome Life's Obstacles and Live in Victory
1-933188-03-0   978-1-9331880-3-4

The race of life is often run through the difficult terrain
of hardship, challenges, and conflict. In *Secrets of the
Second Mile*, Mark Crow combines his own life's experiences with biblical principles to share how you are
designed to finish the race of life—victoriously!

Extraordinary Living
1-933188-51-0   978-1-933188-51-5

Learn who God is, understand the depth and purpose
of His love, and see how extraordinary your life can be!

Unfold   Live Recorded Music
CD 1-9331882-3-5   DVD 1-9331882-2-7
CD 978-1-9331882-3-2   DVD 978-1-9331882-2-5

Allow the Holy Spirit to touch your life with songs
of healing, deliverance, and praise as you join Victory
Church in a live worship-filled atmosphere.